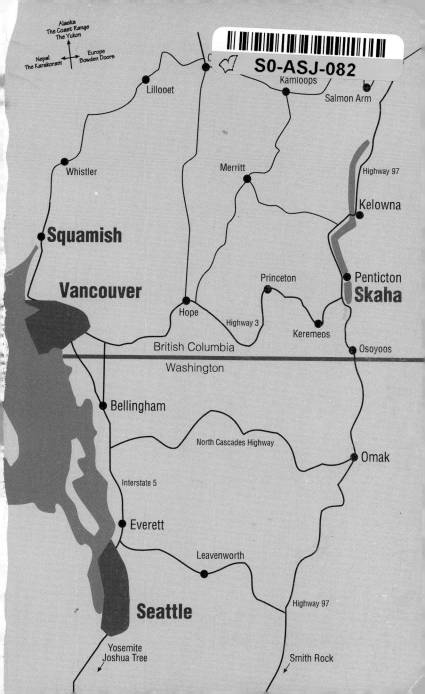

Robin Barley on Doctor Crow

The Climbers' Guide to

SKAHA

Kevin McLane

1993

Merlin Productions Inc

Squamish BC

The Climbers' Guide to Skaha

© Kevin McLane 1993

ISBN 0-9696201-1-X

Printed and bound in Canada

Printing: Hignell Printing Ltd, Winnipeg Manitoba.
Film Output: WYSIWYG Graphics Inc. Vancouver British Columbia.

All photos and graphics by the author except as noted.

Front cover photo: *Howie Richardson on The Plum Line.*
Back cover photos: *An unclimbed crack somewhere at Skaha.*
                          (inset) Robin Barley on Doctor Crow

Private property.
Descriptions to climbs and approach trails do not indicate or imply a legal right of public access.

Now read this!
Rockclimbing is a dangerous activity carrying a significant risk of personal injury or death, and should only be undertaken with a full understanding of all inherent risks. At any given time, the descriptions contained in this guide may not reflect the circumstances of a particular climb. This book is only a guide to the climbs, a composite of opinions from many sources, some of which may not be accurate. It must always be used in conjunction with the exercise of experience, appropriate tuition and careful judgement.

Merlin Productions Inc
Box 5181 Squamish BC Canada V0N 3G0

This book is dedicated to

Derek and Jill Salter

of Okanagan Falls

for the outstanding hospitality they have shown

to so many climbers. They made the exploration

of the crags at Skaha a special time for all.

Table of Contents

Introduction

The development of rockclimbing opportunities in the southern Okanagan is one of the most important events to have occurred in many years in the sport in Canada. The name *'Skaha'*, derived from the beautiful lake beside the city of Penticton, has become synonomous with ever-increasing amounts of fine climbing on fifty crags which offer routes to suit every taste and level of ability.

"Where is Skaha?", has been a persistent query among climbers during the last few years. The answers, when forthcoming at all, have been various and vague, shrouded by a complex web of approaches, access difficulties and a canny penchant for secrecy among the small band of climbers who have developed the routes. Inevitably the pace of development and interest had escalated to such a degree by 1992 that climbers came whether they knew the answers or not, adding further to the access problems. Clearly the time had come to resolve access issues and unwrap a guidebook to finally remove the mystery.

Activity is centred on the hills and benches rising to the east of Skaha Lake. In all, there are some 50 crags and 260 climbs listed in this guide, only part of the potential which the Okanagan holds. The climbs can be divided into two sections, the main collection of cliffs, accessed from two points within the city limits of Penticton and the four cliffs of the Lambing Grounds further to the south. Two small crags, Roadside Cliff and Lakeside Cliff, complete the picture. Penticton at the north end of Skaha Lake and Okanagan Falls at the south end provide all the required amenities. The cliffs require approach hikes of 10 to 45 minutes, over grassy benches, narrow valleys and open forests of ponderosa pine.

The majority of cliffs are on public lands, but access to them over private property has been an issue at the forefront of any discussion about Skaha during the last three years. Evidently, a guide could not be published without resolution of this thorny issue. The situation was addressed with the property owners, and a good solution has come to hand. Along with this comes the responsibility for everyone to abide by the agreements reached. In essence, the main area between the Fortress and Kids' Crag can only be approached from either of two points; Juniper Road to the north and Braesyde to the south. The latter is only some 12 minutes from the Fortress, but requires pay parking. No other approach can be considered acceptable.

The modern era was ushered in when Howie Richardson moved from Vancouver to live in Okanagan Falls in 1987 and began steadily developing the climbs with friends from Vancouver. Since then, Skaha has grown to become a mecca in British Columbia for steep face climbs on a multitude of fierce little crags.

Surely no-one can visit Skaha without taking note of the richness of the wildlife. We share the hills here with many different species of birds, animals and plants, a few of them quite rare. The birdsong in particular adds much to the pleasure of a day on the hill. It is imperative that we respect their needs and leave them in peace.

The rock itself is gneiss, and believed to be among the oldest in British Columbia. It is a delight to climb on, with its steep knobbly texture and generous holds; very modern. It consists of essentially the same components as granite, but its highly metamorphosed state and foliation layers give it a quite different character. Although there are plenty of cracks, it is the profusion of fingery little edges resulting from the layering, which allows such exciting routes. The rock can be friable at first, especially on first ascents, but improves quickly after more use. An interesting feature of the landscape is the wide gully-like trenches and draws which run north to south through the area, a result of glacial action and faulting long ago. The most prominent example is Shady Valley. These gullies offer welcome shade in the summer as well as shelter from the wind.

As a climbing area, Skaha is the antithesis of Squamish, its better known urban relative on the coast. Although lacking the long climbs which are so much a part of the Squamish experience, Skaha offers the climber a tantalising array of crags in a quiet, semi-wilderness situation (and only 15% of the rainfall at Squamish!). The future possibilities are enticing, as more crags remain undeveloped in the region than are in this book.

A few cautionary points to note; There is no water anywhere on the hill, so take your own. Light no fires, the risk of a bushfire spreading into the residential areas is serious. There are no toilet facilities on the hill as yet, and finally, pack all your garbage out.

Good climbing!   *Kevin McLane May 1993.*

How to get to Skaha

WHERE IS SKAHA?

Skaha is an extensive area of hills and crags just south east of the town of Penticton in the Okanagan region of south central British Columbia, 400km east of Vancouver. All of the climbing areas are accessed from South Main Street in Penticton, and the following descriptions apply to that point. See the section on **Parking and Approaches** for more detailed information beyond South Main St.

APPROACHING FROM THE WEST ON HIGHWAY 3

Follow highway 3 through Manning Park to join highway 97 just south of Penticton. Enter the outskirts of the city heading east along the beachfront of Skaha Lake Park. Continue past the beach until the road veers to the north. Go right at the first traffic lights on Yorkton Ave and proceed for 600m to join South Main Street.

APPROACHING FROM THE NORTH ON HIGHWAY 97

When approaching Penticton from the north, highway 97 takes a sharp turn to the left across the Okanagan River Channel (the waterway that links Okanagan Lake to Skaha Lake) and enters the outskirts of the city. After 1.2km turn right at traffic lights onto Channel Parkway (also signed for Railway St), following signs for "Osoyoos" and "Oliver". After 2.7km turn left onto Warren Road, signed for "Industrial Park". Continue for 1.1km to a major intersection with Main Street. Cherry Lane shopping centre is to the right. Turn right, and after 250m turn left onto Kinney Ave, then abruptly right (south) onto South Main Street .

APPROACHING FROM THE UNITED STATES

From Omak in north central Washington State, take highway 97 north across the Canadian border to Penticton. Alternatively, from Interstate 5, exit at Bellingham and cross the Canadian border at Aldergrove to join the Trans Canada Highway. Follow highway 3 through Manning Park to join highway 97 south of Penticton.

SOUTH MAIN STREET

There are two approach roads to the parking places for the main climbing area, both leading off South Main Street. Pineview Road, which leads to Juniper Road, gives the fastest approach to the northern crags. Crescent Hill Road, leading to Valleyview Road and Braesyde Crags, gives the fastest, most pleasant approach to all other crags and is the best starting point for the Skaha Loop Trail.

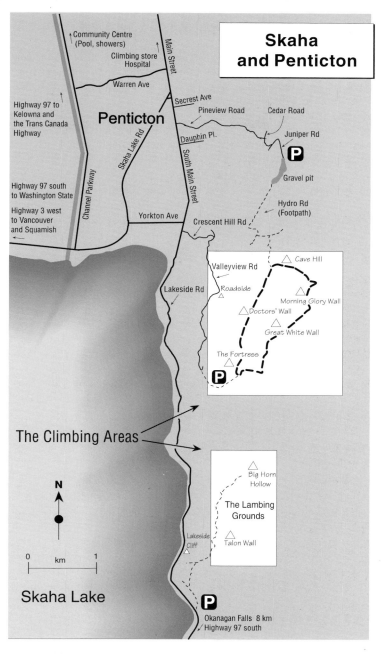

Skaha
and Penticton

Community Centre
(Pool, showers)

Climbing store
Hospital

Main Street

Warren Ave

Highway 97 to
Kelowna and
the Trans Canada
Highway

Secrest Ave

Pineview Road

Cedar Road

Penticton

Juniper Rd

Dauphin Pl.

P

Skaha Lake Rd

South Main Street

Gravel pit

Highway 97 south
to Washington State

Hydro Rd
(Footpath)

Channel Parkway

Highway 3 west
to Vancouver
and Squamish

Yorkton Ave

Crescent Hill Rd

Valleyview Rd

△ Cave Hill

Lakeside Rd

Roadside
△

△
Morning Glory Wall

△ Doctors' Wall

△
Great White Wall

The Fortress
△

P

The Climbing Areas

N

△
Big Horn
Hollow

The Lambing
Grounds

Lakeside
Cliff
△

△
Talon Wall

0   km   1

Skaha Lake

P

Okanagan Falls 8 km
Highway 97 south

4

Parking and Approaches

Parking and access have been contentious issues during the last few years, as the only routes that could be taken into the main climbing area required crossing private property. In the early days from 1987 to 1989, there were few problems, but as the popularity of Skaha increased, the situation became untenable. Recently, the newly formed Skaha Climbers Association has reached agreement with some of the property owners that formally allows access, subject to several reasonable conditions.

There are now two parking areas to choose from, one at the northern end and one at the southern end. The northern approach, from the gravel pit at the end of Juniper Road provides the fastest access to the crags between Chatsworth Edge and Morning Glory Wall. The southern approach from Braesyde Crags on Valleyview Road gives the fastest approach to all other crags and is without doubt the most pleasant starting point for a hike around the Skaha Loop Trail. Under no circumstances should anyone approach from locations along Valleyview Road other than Braesyde, as you will be an unwelcome trespasser on private property.

It is of special note that the new parking area at Braesyde Crags has not only solved a major problem for climbers but also created a fine approach to the crags, being just 12 minutes from the East Face of the Fortress. However, this privilege carries with it the payment of a fee to park at Braesyde, a reasonable request under the circumstances. This can be done on a daily basis, or better still, by purchasing a modestly priced annual pass.

It is essential that all climbers (and hikers) abide by this agreement. If you don't wish to pay, walk in from Juniper Rd. Annual parking passes can be obtained from Ray's Sports Den at 215 Main Street, Penticton. Alternatively, buy a day pass on-site.

VALLEYVIEW ROAD TO BRAESYDE CRAGS PARKING.

Valleyview Road is narrow and winding, so please drive slowly. Turn off South Main Street at Crescent Hill Road and follow it uphill. After about 500m, join Valleyview Road and head south for 1.1km to Roadside Cliff. 400m beyond, the view opens out over the surrounding farmland. Althought the road becomes a single lane from here, it is a public highway. Go down the right hand fork at the junction with Valleyview Ranch, and continue for another 600m, avoiding turns to the right. At this point, the road begins to switchback to the left. Do not proceed into the switch-back, but turn right down a partly hidden gravel road which leads to a parking area in an idyllic flat meadow below Braesyde Crags.

PINEVIEW ROAD TO JUNIPER ROAD PARKING.

Exit off South Main Street onto Pineview Road. This is a suburban street, so please use caution. As you climb up the winding hill, avoid turns to the left or right. After 1.3km, turn right onto Cedar Road at an obvious junction. 200m further, turn left onto Juniper Road, which leads in 300m to a large open area at the north end of a gravel pit, 1.8km from South Main Street. Park here on the left at the entrance. **Do not park in the gravel pit or drive across it!**

THE LAMBING GROUNDS.

This climbing area is 6km south of Penticton and parking is just off Lakeside Road. See that section in the guide for more information.

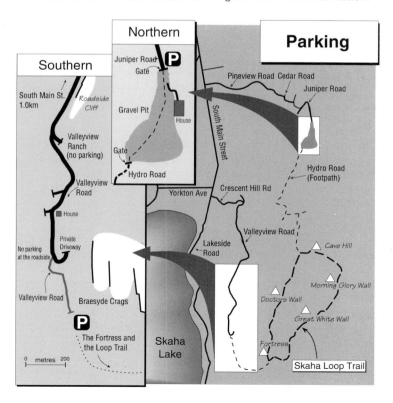

How to use this Guide

The geography of the crags and the trails in the Skaha area can be difficult to grasp, so a few minutes spent reading this section will help gain an understanding of the way the information is laid out.

- ◆ Use the Table of Contents for page references to the crags.

- ◆ The small icon beside each route name in the text indicates the page where the photograph or map of the climb is located.

- ◆ The Skaha Loop Trail is used as the means of describing access to most of the crags in the guide. Get familiar with this trail system and life will be easier.

- ◆ "Left" and "Right" assume the climber to be facing the rock.

- ◆ Pitch lengths should be used as a guide only, and refer to the amount of rope required.

- ◆ Rating stars give an indication of the quality of a climb. Three stars for the very best, two for excellent climbs, one for good climbs and no stars for the rest.

- ◆ Occasional reference is made to fixed gear where it can be a convenient help for route finding.

- ◆ The designations N M F beside the route names refer to the type of protection available on the climb. N for natural gear throughout; M for mixed natural and fixed gear; F for all fixed gear. Note that fixed pro. may include pins as well as bolts.

- ◆ Many climbs have received few if any repeat ascents, so caution is advised when assessing grades and protection.

- ◆ The map opposite illustrates the way in which the descriptions of the climbs are planned, and how they flow through the book.

Abbreviations

N	Natural protection only	TR	Top-rope climb (not led)
F	Fixed protection only	2p	Number of pitches
M	Mixed protection	m	Metres in length
FA	First Ascent	km	Kilometres
FFA	First Free Ascent	FP	Fixed pin
[OS]	On-sight first ascent	c.	Approximate date
(Alts)	Alternate leads	qd	Quickdraws
(2pa)	Points of aid used	(p1)	pitch (credits)

Symbols

— — — — The Skaha Loop Trail	**247** Topo route numbers	Crags
- - - - - - - Good trails	Route hidden	
· · · · · · · · Other trails	Belay station	Scree slopes
123 Photo page icon	Rappel station	Copse of trees
△ Hilltops	**P** Parking areas	

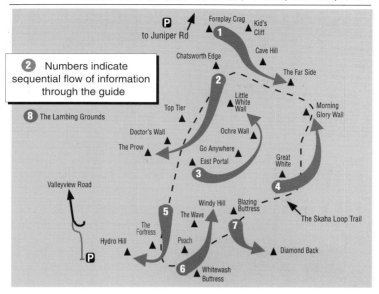

On ticks, snakes, and suchlike...

TICKS... These flat, round insects about 3-4mm in diameter can be a skin pest in the early spring, lurking in tall grass and low shrubs. Inspect yourself and **ALL** clothing daily. They can be removed if stubborn with tweezers by gently twisting or using irritants like gasoline. Disease is rare but not to be taken lightly.

SNAKES... Although seldom seen, rattlesnakes live around here and take the greatest exception to being stepped on. Otherwise, the likelihood of being zapped is remote. A bite is painful, but rarely fatal. In the event, do not apply a tourniquet or cut the wound, just get to a hospital as soon as possible.

POISON IVY... Poison ivy may be encountered in some areas, a low plant with 3 glossy, bright green leaves and white berries. Don't handle it or drag a rope through it as you'll get a nasty rash. It is easy to avoid, but Calamine lotion helps if you get nailed.

HUNTERS... A threatened sub-species. Don't dress like a sheep.

WASPS... A species of wasp is sometimes found drifting around aimlessly in sunny corners. They usually appear uninterested in climbers, but don't rely on it. Incidents have been rare.

8

The Skaha Loop Trail

The Skaha Loop Trail is a circular route around the main climbing area that passes close to most of the crags and all of the popular ones. Aside from being an excellent way to understand the topography of the area and gain access to the cliffs, it is a first class hike in its own right, traversing open benchlands, dense thickets, deep canyons and fine open stands of tall pine forest. Throughout the route, there are regular extensive views across the surrounding hills, Okanagan Lake to the north, Penticton and Skaha Lake. Depending on speed and inclination, allow 2-2½ hrs return from the car. Climbing skills are not required, except when descending from Valleyview Ridge down into Shady Valley where exposed scrambling may be a bit too much for some hikers. An alternative is described which does not involve climbing. At the present time, parts of the trail are well worn but there are sections where the route is indistinct. This will change over time.

APPROACHING THE LOOP TRAIL FROM JUNIPER ROAD

From the parking area on Juniper Road, walk south across the gravel pit to Hydro Road in the southwest corner. There is a cable gate at this point. Private residential properties border Hydro Road on the west side, so do not wander in that direction. Follow the undulating road less than 10 minutes until it turns left down into a draw and crosses below overhead powerlines. The road rises up again to a crest. Just beyond the crest turn left onto another, narrower dirt road. Hike up this road for about 100m until a wide trail is clearly seen veering off sharply to the right. Follow it steadily uphill as the trees thin out and the view opens across the Lake. After about 3 minutes, the trail reaches a flat bench on the left. At this point, an inconspicuous path turns sharply back to the left. After another 50m or so, turn south to enter a thicket in a hidden trench. Another few minutes along here leads to **Shortcut Cliff** on the left. The trail continues its gently rising traverse out of the trench and up the hillside for another 100m, then climbs more steeply up to a crest and a view of the west face of **Cave Hill. Chatsworth Edge** is now to the right, facing east. Head south along the crest for 50m, then step down a short distance to the base of the crag at its northern end. 25 minutes from the car.

APPROACHING THE LOOP TRAIL FROM VALLEYVIEW ROAD

From the Braesyde parking area, follow wide trail uphill to the southeast. Beyond the hill, turn left up the steep hillside to reach the flat bench south-east of the Fortress. Head 50m across this bench then down to a stand of tall pine trees in Shady Valley and the junction with the Loop Trail.

THE LOOP TRAIL DESCRIBED

This description assumes starting from Braesyde parking area on Valleyview Road, from which a counter-clockwise route is taken.

THE FORTRESS SOUTH TO GREAT WHITE WALL

From the stand of tall pine trees at the south end of Shady Valley, a trail heads northeast up the hillside to the edge of the talus below **White Slab,** then turns east onto a large flat bench in front of **Peach Buttress.** At the toe of the obvious arete, turn left up a slab and continue northward to more benches above. After another 50m or so, step down a small rock shelf, turn right for 30m then left along a bench with a low rock wall on the left. A tall, red snag marks the junction with an old road on the right, rising up steeply to the south end of **Elusive Edge** and a junction with the trail from the Wave and Red Tail Wall. Continue northward up the main valley passing below Elusive Edge. (for Diamond Back, go right down into the bottom and take the trail heading east from there). Beyond Elusive Edge, the trail makes a rising traverse up the hillside, **and Blazing Buttress** can be seen behind the trees to the left. The trail continues up steeply right of Blazing Buttress and then over open slabs to the scenic benches south of the Great White Wall. Head northeast past the cliffs on the left to continue along the Loop Trail, otherwise keep left for the climbs on **Great White Wall.** 20 minutes.

GREAT WHITE WALL TO MORNING GLORY

Contour around the south end of **Great White Wall**, heading east past the inviting crack of **Grassy Glades.** Walk 100m northeast up a slabby slope to the top of a crest, beyond which is a deep gully. Head north from here, passing below a prominent south facing shoulder of rock, **Far Away. Easter Island** can be seen to its left. Scramble down over a small boulderfield then strike out right onto a large slabby bench. The south end of **Morning Glory** is now 200m to the north. To reach the climbs, head north along the benches until the obvious slash of *Squeezy Stomach* comes into view. Head left now, passing a dense thicket of small trees. Scramble up some steps 50m south of *Flying Flowers* to reach the terrace from which the climbs begin. 20 minutes from Great White Wall.

MORNING GLORY TO CHATSWORTH

The terrace below the climbs runs the full length of Morning Glory Wall. North of a wide vegetated draw, remain on the lower bench until a short scramble up some steps leads to a meadow north of the cliff. Turn west across a flat grassy saddle. 150m later, the **Far Side** is reached. Continue downhill passing **Stove Cliff** to reach the gully on the east side of **Cave Hill.** Traverse below the South Face and trend left down into Shady Valley. A trail leads in 100m or so to the north end of **Chatsworth Edge.** 30 minutes.

CHATSWORTH EDGE TO DOCTORS' WALL

From the northern end of Chatsworth Edge, walk along the base of the cliff, or the ridge crest above, to a wide col at its south end. Continue south for 50m and follow the crest of Valleyview Ridge. The ridge continues beyond to the summit of the **Top Tier**. At the cairn, step left down from the crest of the ridge, past a pine tree to a long parallel ledge. Walk south along this ledge and scramble down to the treed slope which leads into Shady Valley. Alternatively, scramble steeply down directly onto a lower ledge (see overview photo p39) at the top of the Screeching Wall. Walk south along this ledge for 50m to a short rock step which leads down to the treed slope and the bottom of Shady Valley. (For the **Top Tier**, turn up to the right at this point). The main trail now descends into the bottom of Shady Valley. For **Screeching Wall** and **Maternal Wall**, trails fork off to the northward from here. **Doctors' Wall, Blipvert Tower,** and **East Portal** are reached in a few minutes. *If the scrambling down from Valleyview Ridge is unwelcome,* it is possible to avoid it by a different, albeit less interesting route. From the col at the south end of **Chatsworth Edge** head down a short trail into Shady Valley. Follow the open rocky bed of the gully, generally on its east side. It becomes a deep, narrow canyon as it passes underneath the **Screeching Wall.** The trail is rough at present but will improve over time. The **Doctors' Wall** area is reached a few minutes later. 20 minutes.

DOCTORS' WALL TO THE FORTRESS

From **Doctors' Wall,** head south over short steps and open slabs parallel with Shady Valley. After a few minutes, the trail rises up to meet the first rocks of **The Fortress.** Keep left at the first step and join the north end of a narrowing terrace which descends to the base of the of **Red Tail Wall Lower Tier.** Just past the **Lower Tier,** the trail descends down into the bed of Shady Valley to **Another Buttress.** Beyond here, the trail becomes rocky and passes through a narrowing to reach the climbs on the **Corridor.** 50m further, the trail rises up to the wide sloping terrace at the base of the **East Face.** Just before the southern end of the **East Face,** trails drop back down to the grove of tall pine trees in Shady Valley. 15 minutes.

MORE TRAILS:

A number of good trails exist between crags inside the Loop, notably the trails from Red Tail Wall to Elusive Edge and from Doctors' Wall to Ochre Wall and Great White Wall.

THE SUMMIT OF THE FORTRESS

A hike to the summit of the Fortress is a worthwhile side trip off the main Loop Trail. Where the trail from Doctors' Wall meets the first rocks at the north end of Red Tail Wall, scramble up the rocky step and head up over open terrain for the summit, negotiating the odd rock step along the way. The view over the lake and hills is well worth it and takes only a few minutes extra.

11

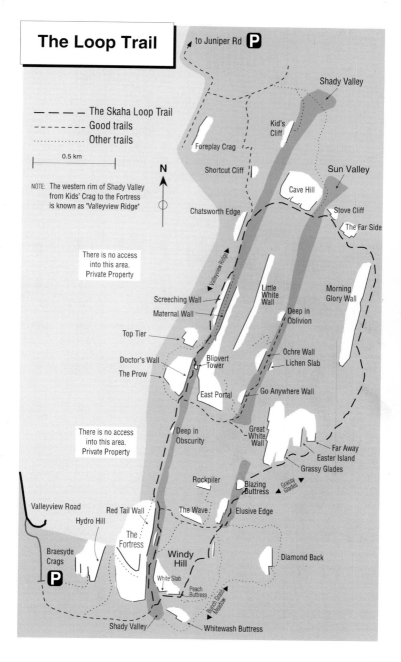

The Loop Trail

to Juniper Rd 🅿

Shady Valley

— — — The Skaha Loop Trail
– – – – – Good trails
············· Other trails

|— 0.5 km —|

N

NOTE: The western rim of Shady Valley
from Kids' Crag to the Fortress
is known as "Valleyview Ridge"

Kid's Cliff

Foreplay Crag

Shortcut Cliff

Sun Valley

Cave Hill

Stove Cliff

The Far Side

Chatsworth Edge

Valleyview Ridge

Screeching Wall

Maternal Wall

Top Tier

Doctor's Wall

The Prow

Little White Wall

Deep in Oblivion

Morning Glory Wall

Blipvert Tower

Ochre Wall

Lichen Slab

East Portal

Go Anywhere Wall

There is no access
into this area.
Private Property

There is no access
into this area.
Private Property

Deep in Obscurity

Great White Wall

Far Away

Easter Island

Grassy Glades

Rockpiler

Blazing Buttress

Grassy Glades

Valleyview Road

Red Tail Wall

Hydro Hill

The Fortress

The Wave

Elusive Edge

Windy Hill

Diamond Back

Braesyde Crags

🅿

White Slab

Peach Buttress

Bunch Grass Meadow

Shady Valley

Whitewash Buttress

12

Ethics, Style and that kind of stuff...

To non-climbers and climbers who have no taste for the peculiarities of making first ascents, the seemingly endless discussions on the merits of the style employed, and the quality of the resulting routes can seem rather bizarre. Whilst we debate whether we should place a bolt here or there, or we ponder the values of natural protection, millions of people across the world face starvation and war every day. As we consider the implications of retro-bolting, the ozone layer slowly disappears. Nonetheless, the debate rages amongst this particular tribe of *Homo sapiens* where sport, risk, adventure and art must co-exist on the rock.

The efforts of a few have a profound effect on the habits of the many. It is a curious fact that only a tiny percentage of climbers, armed with an unusual quantity of skill, foresight, and energy regularly engage in making first ascents. Of the 260 or so climbs in this guide, about 60% were established by 9 climbers, of which almost half were put up by just 2 individuals.

The two basic methods of establishing a new route are both practised at Skaha: Most popular is rappel inspection, cleaning and pre-placement of any fixed gear. Some climbers are happy with a cursory glance at the holds and a quick scrub, whereas others conduct a microscopic study of each nubbin and undertake meticulous preparation. The second method is on-sight leading from the ground up, with fixed gear placed on lead if necessary and cleaning done later (a third of the climbs were done this way).

The early years of development have given rise to plenty of shenanigans on the crags as the competition for new routes heated up. Given the amount of unclimbed rock in the region, many more climbers will undoubtedly wish to try their hand at first ascents. In anticipation of this and the publication of the first guidebook, there has been much canvassing of opinion to seek a consensus as to what climbers envision for the future. This is reflected in this list of conventions. The rest is up to you...

- Preserve the rock in as natural a condition as possible. This will minimise our impact and leave the best possible legacy for other climbers in the future. People will be climbing here long after we are all gone. Give them a chance to enjoy the rock as we do.

- You have the freedom to choose your own style of establishing a first ascent, but that freedom brings responsibilities and limitations. We don't own the crags, we share them. Respect for your own approach is more likely to be shown if you demonstrate tolerance of others.

◆ Respect the projects that others are working on, whether they be hard or easy. Don't be greedy by taking on too many yourself. Set a time to accomplish your goal, and work at it consistently. Some climbers like to mark their projects in some way, so don't remove quick-draws if present. If you abandon it, tell others.

◆ No placing of bolts beside natural protection. Respect and encourage the diversity of climbing styles.

◆ Don't add more bolts or convenience belay stations after a climb has been established, and don't remove any either. This has been a most nettlesome business in the past. Climbers are a touchy lot.

◆ Think carefully before placing bolts or fixed belay stations within reach of an existing climb. Rarely is it acceptable.

◆ No chipping. This is a despised and selfish activity, considered to be illegal in the Parks. Leave the next generation an inspiration.

◆ Place bolts with foresight as to their best position, others will either curse your folly or enjoy your good judgement. Not every-one is seven feet tall or a dwarf. Stainless steel bolts are much preferred for corrosion resistance. Use bolts and fixed pins as sparingly as possible (It's cheaper that way), with camouflage.

◆ If you put up an easy route without natural protection, spare a thought for beginners who may quake at the prospect of huge run-outs. Save them for harder routes.

◆ Try to do a decent cleaning job, whether before your ascent or after. Your work will be appreciated.

New Routes and Future Editions

Describing the crags and their locations is not always a simple matter, so please try to be as clear as possible when recording new routes or crags. Fame and glory will assuredly follow, but only if others can find your route.

There are two ways to keep the world informed. A new route book is kept at the climbing store, Ray's Sports Den at 215 Main Street in downtown Penticton (493-1216), and is the best place to record any new routes and keep yourself up to date with what is happening. It will be appreciated by all if you would record the details as accurately as possible. Please state the grade, ascent credits, length, and the kind of protection used. When developing new crags not listed in this guide, explain the exact location and how to find it (if you want anyone else to). If you can't get to the new route book, please send a card listing all the details to Kevin McLane at Box 5181 Squamish BC V0N 3G0.

14

Protection equipment

Skaha climbs are mostly face routes of one kind or another, with the highly featured rock lending itself well to modern protection equipment. Classic cracks add further variety. Wire nuts of all kinds and camming devices, especially the smaller sizes work well. Many climbs have fixed protection and require quickdraws only. The most popular routes usually have rappel stations on top. The rock quality in general is good, but some climbs suffer from friable edges until they see more traffic. In these situations it pays to be prudent, especially if you are belaying.

The Grading System

The grading system is the Tahquitz Decimal system, used across North America. Technical rockclimbs which require the use of protection equipment are graded on an ascending scale from 5.0 to the current highest standard of 5.14. The hardest climbs in this guide are 5.12. Grades from 5.10 upward are further subdivided into a,b,c, and d categories, a concept first developed in Yosemite Valley in 1973. It must be borne in mind that Skaha is a relatively new climbing area, so **discrepancies are certain on some climbs between the currently stated grade and the level at which they will likely settle in the future.** Many climbs have not yet received a second ascent. On the more popular routes, however, the grades are generally consistent.

International Grading Systems

Canada/USA	German	British	French	Australian
5.9	6	5a	5c	18
5.10a	6+	5b / E1	5c+	19
5.10b	7-	E2	6a	
5.10c			6a+	20
5.10d	7	5c	6b	21
5.11a	7+	E3	6b+	22
5.11b	8-	6a / E4	6c	
5.11c	8	E5	6c+	23
5.11d			7a	24
5.12a	8+	6b	7a+	
5.12b	9-	E6	7b	25
5.12c	9	6c	7b+	26
5.12d		E7	7c	27
5.13a	9+		7c+	28
5.13b	10-	7a	8a	29
5.13c	10	E8	8a+	30
5.13d				

Access and Private Property

Access into the climbing area has been a longstanding issue of importance to all climbers and hikers. The majority of the cliffs of interest are on public lands, but there are several private properties bordering the climbing area, some of which climbers cross to reach the cliffs. A set of guidelines for access and behaviour have been developed between the Skaha Climbers Association and the affected property owners. It is essential that all climbers take the time to understand these reasonable limitations and put them into practice. This is a very important issue, as the future of climbing here will depend on the positive cooperation of all climbers and the goodwill of property owners.

The two access routes into the main area, from Juniper Road and Braesyde Crags on Valleyview Road both cross private property. The respective owners have been generous in allowing access to climbers, subject to several reasonable conditions. Continued usage is at their discretion, so travel wisely. At these two designated parking areas, signs have been erected to inform climbers and hikers of parking, access and land management concerns. Please read them and observe the requirements.

Use of the Braesyde Crags parking area, the best place for reaching most of the crags and the Skaha Loop Trail, requires paid parking. If you don't wish to pay, walk in from Juniper Road.

The Lambing Grounds were purchased by the Government of BC to provide secure terrain for Big Horn Sheep to breed. The public have access, but there are concerns that the presence of too many climbers may cause the sheep to leave, a matter which is currently under study. It is possible the area may be closed for a period of time early in the season. If that should occur, please observe any posted signs.

Please observe the following conditions

- ◆ No fires or smoking. Local residents have great concerns over the potential of bush fires.
- ◆ No garbage. You carry it in - You carry it out.
- ◆ Drive cautiously through residential areas.
- ◆ Park only in the designated places.
- ◆ Minimise your impact and trail erosion.
- ◆ Pay the fee at Braesyde if you park there.
- ◆ Be courteous and considerate to local residents.

Climbing History

Climbers have been active throughout the Okanagan for many years, certainly since the late 1960's, but their numbers were few and ascents largely unrecorded. In the area covered by this guide prior to 1987, only the cliffs of Lakeside and Roadside saw some limited activity, the main climbing areas were untouched. The subterranean descent inside Cave Hill attracted Penticton area locals from time to time, notably the boy scouts, and at least one climb was done on the huge rambling wall of MacIntyre Bluff.

During Easter 1982, Howie Richardson, Chris Murrell and Kevin McLane spent a day climbing at Roadside Cliff, and hiked up to inspect the Prow. Its formidable appearance was quite daunting and there were doubts as to how solid the rock would be. After that day at Roadside, the three of them studied the hillside across Skaha Lake, noting the numerous crags that were evident and became convinced there was much that was worth exploring.

1987

The chance came in 1987 when Richardson moved with his family to live in Okanagan Falls. In April, he and Bob Cuthbert set off to further investigate the area. The complex topography for which Skaha is well known became evident as they picked their way along Shady Valley past Doctors' Wall and on up to Great White. The weather turned to snow and sleet and they headed back to the north, past the unremarkable little Stove Cliff where they paused long enough to climb *Primus*. With that inauspicious first climb, the modern era of climbing arrived at Skaha.

Finding climbing partners was the first obstacle for Richardson to overcome, as all eyes at that time were firmly on Squamish. Dave Hetherington was successfully persuaded, and the two were occasionally accompanied by Bob Cuthbert. The three ex-Brits explored the cliffs at length, ticking off many fine little climbs at Chatsworth Edge, and leaving their mark on half a dozen other cliffs. Names such as *Gem Quality, Uncut* and *Diamond in the Rough* expressed their feelings at the exclusive hegemony they enjoyed. Great White was breached in the summer, with *Dryathlon*, quickly followed by the stunning dihedral of *Gang Bang*, accompanied on that occasion by Chris Murrell and Dave McCashin. A week later saw the first visit from Rick Cox, who repeated *Gang Bang*.

1988

By the spring of 1988, the scene was set for a faster pace. Hetherington led the classic *Double Exposure* at East Portal, an outstanding cracked ramp up an overhanging wall, while Richardson led the big crack of *Conductress on the Number 19*, the first Fortress climb on Red Tail Wall.

In May, Richardson set about the huge arete on the Prow, one of the most dramatic lines at Skaha. With Mark Gardiner, he led the first pitch on-sight, an overhanging tour de force of jamming and exposure which went at an amazingly easy grade of 5.10b. He returned with a borrowed drill to place a station, the first usage of a power drill on the crags at Skaha,

Two weeks later, accompanied by Mark Gardiner and an enthused Robin Barley enjoying his first visit, he finished the route, *Slowpitch,* up the steep and exciting top pitch. Future possibilities now seemed endless.

Although intriguing rumours had begun circulating on the coast about a climbing area near Penticton, it was only the indefatigable Barley, also an ex-Brit, who ventured east to see what it was all about. McLane and Murrell had remained tight-lipped which made Barley suspicious that something was up. After his first visit he returned three weeks later, this time accompanied by his son Nick and Mark Petersen. They spied the crackline which Richardson had cleaned at the south end of a steep impressive cliff near East Portal and proceeded to climb it under the mistaken assumption that it was *Double Exposure.* Barley contritely named the route *Doctor Crow* in recognition of Richardson's recent doctorate in biology. Barley and Petersen were both physicians, so the name Doctors' Wall was appropriately given. Barley was now in full flight, and was to have a major impact on the development of the cliffs over the following years.

Three other notable routes of that year were led by Richardson. *Assholes of August,* the classic crack at the north end of Red Tail Wall; *PhS,* the big off-width crack on Doctors' Wall, climbed on-sight, and the first airy pitch of *Horsehoes, Handgrenades and Hoffwidths* at Great White.

1989

This was a year of rapid development. In addition to Rick Cox, a new force had begun scoping for routes, Gary Wolkoff and Sue Chaytor, all residents of the northern Okanagan. Between themselves, Barley and Richardson, almost 50 new routes were put up. Wolkoff and Chaytor had discovered the long golden edge of Morning Glory at the eastern fringe of the main climbing area, and climbed some cracks and chimneys, notably *Flying Flowers.* In May, they returned with Cox, who led the daunting *Supercharger* .

The impressive wide arete on Great White beside *Fun Run* attracted the attention of Barley, and he set about it, climbing ground up as usual. A broken hold sent him off on a 20 metre fall, almost hitting the ground. Bloody but unbowed, he tried again, this time veering off to the right up a distinct line of thin cracks to join *Fun Run*, creating the appropriately named *Flying Yorkshireman* . The big arete would wait another year.

Red Tail Wall at the Fortress could be seen clearly in profile from the Doctors' Wall, but less obvious was the East Face. Richardson trotted along to it one day in September to re-inspect the lines he was eyeing up, and to his disappointment discovered Rick Cox hard at work on a line of right trending grooves which he named *Et Tu Brutus.* Cox also climbed *Itching to Climb* that day, and for his pains got a nasty dose of poison ivy rash. The previous weekend, Cox had been climbing in Hydro Hill gully, and just went for "a look around the corner" and discovered the potential of the East Face, He wasted no time returning to start ticking routes. Richardson wasted no more time either, quickly returning to climb *The Plum Line*, a superb face climb capped by a small roof. It went at an amazingly easy grade of 5.10a. A week earlier on Hydro Hill, Sue Chaytor led *Low Resistance* and Wolkoff led *High Voltage*, both of them excellent short cracks. In October, Richardson cleaned what was to be *Storming the Ramparts*, but was unable to complete the final moves. He handed the rope over to a sixteen year old Nick Barley, who despatched it. A month earlier, Nick had made the first ascent of the 5.11a *Unethical* at the Doctors' Wall. In October McLane, another aging ex-Brit, led *Elysian Fields* on the south face of the Prow. Climbing with Richardson, he reached a point just below the big fault.

1990

This was a year in which there was a big leap forward in the standard of difficulty. The Victoria Day weekend marked the arrival of a new team from the coast, the lanky figures of Dean Hart and Randy Atkinson. Initially they came just to see what the fuss was all about, but quickly became hooked by the potential and returned almost every weekend that spring. The hardest climb was 5.11a and the steeper walls had barely been touched, easy prey for the right climbers. Hart was to establish a number of superb climbs over the next two years and helped raise the game to a new level.

Barley finished the formidable big arete at Great White on the Easter weekend, but not without using some aid. He returned in May with Peter Shackleton, who was able to free-climb the route, *Test of the Ironman*, but took several falls and rests in the process. As he repeatedly winged through the air, Hart and Atkinson were psyching up for their chance to try. Hart made fine work of an on-sight flash the same day. Considerable debate ensued as to what constituted a "free" ascent, pointing to a clear division in style which was to become more evident later.

The spring of 1990 was a turning point in the concept of how new routes should best be done. The on-sight approach began to lose its lustre for Barley after his big fall the previous year, and Atkinson had a big fright with loose rock on an early attempt at *The Leaner*. A general unease over the quality of the rock took hold, and top-down inspection, whilst never questioned previously, became the accepted way of doing new routes for the activists at that time. The trend to the open face climbs accelerated the notion that many bolts were going to be needed.

Down at the Fortress, Wolkoff, climbing with Bert Marchand scored a very impressive two pitch route with *Primal Dream* at the edge of the East Face and the Corridor. The lower wall is a constant test of ingenuity. The tremendous crackline on the wall left of *Gang Bang* saw an attempt by Barley in May. Climbing on-sight he failed to master the difficulties of the overhanging crack. Hart later succeeded in June, but not before placing a line of bolts up the route beside the crack. Thus was born *Wings of Desire*. The bolting was a portent of the coming controversy over climbing ethics, which unfortunately threw a shadow over Hart's fine effort.

19

Atkinson nabbed the spectacular corner at Braesyde Crag with Barley and Josh Korman, *Cry Freedom*. In July two superb 5.11d's were done at Doctors' Wall. The big arching corner right of *Doctor Crow* fell to Hart, *The Future is Now* and Larry Ostrander, a lone invader from the Rockies, scored a coup with *Doctor Megatrip*, up the centre of the overhanging wall right of *PhS*. Along with *Wings of Desire*, they now make a trio of highly sought-after testpieces. 1990 was becoming a great year.

In the summer, Korman climbed the striking 40m arete on Braesyde Crag, *Sparky Bites,* giving Skaha its first 5.12. For his trouble, he was bitten on the arse by Sparky himself, an irate local dog. In September, there was a flurry of activity as a growing band of climbers began scoping for first ascents. At one point four or five power drills were at work simultaneously. New Zealander John McCallum finished *Acid Test* at Great White, a demanding climb up a slim overlap which joined *Test of the Ironman* below its crux. Dan Jackson put up *Snakeskin Tracksuit* at the Ochre Wall, still the hardest route at Skaha. Sari Cox led *It's About Time* at Go Anywhere Wall, the only first ascent by a woman other than Sue Chaytor. Andy Kruger led the hard face climb *Peaches* and Peter Shackleton climbed the intimidating *Eerily Hanging Out* at Great White. Finally, Lindsay Eltis made a foray with a lead of *Misdiagnosed* at Doctors' Wall.

1991

This was a quiet year which saw only 25 new routes but a marked increase in visitors. Richardson was building a house so he was effectively out of the picture. In April, the dark, beetling overhangs of Screeching Wall were the scene of a formidable route worked out by Hart, *Isis*, while on the Fortress East Face, a fine top pitch of sustained 5.11 face climbing was added to *Siege Machine* by seventeen year old Robin Shackleton when it proved too much for his father to lead.

Doctors' Wall was rapidly becoming the sorting ground for climbers anxious to repeat the harder routes. Its sheltered aspect in Shady Valley, unlike Great White's bold upthrust, attracted climbers escaping the heat and the wind, and to enjoy the sociable banter at the base. The wide and sunny East Face of the Fortress was the preferred cliff for more moderate 5.10's.

Perplexed climbers were becoming a common sight around this time at the base of the cliffs, poring over a few dog-eared sheets of tenth generation photocopies, Richardson's legendary list of new routes which had somehow found its way out into the world. Never intended as a guide to such a complex area, it was pressed into service as such, and many a lost climber was seen at the Fortress trying to find *Doctor Crow* or *Gang Bang*.

There had been few problems over access to the cliffs until now, but as the number of climbers grew steadily so did the concerns of local residents at having climbers traipsing over their property. The majority of the crags were on crown land, but the perimeter of the area was all private property.

There was a reluctant acceptance by Skaha regulars that easy access direct from Roadside Cliff was now a thing of the past. Access from the Juniper Road gravel pit in the north, and Smythe Drive in the south became the usual approaches in 1991, but many climbers were unaware of these details and came from all directions. In fact, many climbers preferred to avoid Skaha altogether because of these difficulties. Both approaches were (and still are) privately owned, so that situation could not last either.

The growing access problem and friction over the competition for new routes convinced Cox and Wolkoff to explore an extensive area to the south of the main body of cliffs, known as the Lambing Grounds. In fact, they were responsible for half of the climbs done in 1991. A huge rambling cliff, Talon Wall, attracted their attention and they proceeded to establish several excellent routes in the 5.10 - 5.11 range. Of particular note is *STP*, *Raptor's Prey*, *The Griffin* and *Thunderbird,* which is the area's longest climb. The Lambing Grounds hold considerable possibilities for future development.

1992

Word was spreading fast. The number of visiting climbers, almost all from the lower mainland of BC rose dramatically in 1992. Despite the lack of accurate information and the still-unresolved access issue, people came to see for themselves what Skaha was all about. Americans were conspicuous by their absence, handicapped even more by the lack of information.

The year began with many climbers now aware of the potential for new routes, and ended with over eighty more established, most of them in the Fall. April saw the arrival of another formidable Barley, Tony, the younger half of the legendary Barley brothers team of 1960's fame in Britain. Although invited to Skaha to climb the classics with his brother Robin, in typical Barley style he preferred new routes instead. Climbing with his son, Tim, he put up half a dozen that weekend, including a bold on-sight solo of *Little Darling* at Windy Hill. Robin continued his assault on the East Face of the Fortress, the best of his work being *Mortal Combat* with visiting Brit John Jones and *Fearful in Battle* with Guy Edwards.

Meanwhile, not to be outdone by the competition, Cox and Wolkoff scored a fine coup with their ascent of *Ready to Strike* at Diamond Back, a splendid classic corner carved out of the cliff. While they were on the route, they watched a curious rattlesnake make itself comfortable in their pack.

A much loved feature for Skaha climbing regulars was the camping scene at Derek Salter's field. Howie Richardson's father-in-law, Derek was generous in allowing Howie's friends to camp on his idyllic setting on the shore of Skaha Lake. Holiday weekends were especially memorable; kids played while bold tales were told around the bonfire and news of the latest exploits spread fast. Derek and his wife Jill played a notable part in creating a fine camaraderie in the early years of development.

By this time about twenty climbs, for a variety of reasons, had been the subject of retro-bolting, whether for mid-pitch top-roping stations for single ropes, to avoid placing gear or to improve protection. As this trend was accelerating, friction over the preferred Skaha style increased noticeably and at one point it seemed that bolts were being chopped as fast as they were going in. At the heart of the matter was the balance between adventure and sport, with the focal point the drilling of bolts beside natural protection.

Thanksgiving weekend saw 50 climbers and their families camping at Derek Salter's field, resulting in many repeats of the harder routes and seventeen new routes. Sig Isaac, Greg Child and Greg Foweraker all climbed *Acid Test*. Heads turned when Isaac made a bold lead of *Wings of Desire* with only natural protection, not even the fixed pins, adding more fuel to the debate over style. Isaac had the advantage of having previously climbed the route. Richardson was now back in action and not to be outdone on his home turf. By the end of the year he had produced a dozen more routes and remarkably, had been involved in one third of all the climbs at Skaha. Hugh Lennie became firmly encamped at Skaha in the Fall and spent several weeks patiently scrubbing the smooth northern expanse of Red Tail Wall left of *Assholes of August*. He produced a crop of elegant and popular face climbs, notably *Treasure in the Lichen*.

At the end of the season, the Skaha Climbers Association was formed, and minds were concentrated on finding solutions to the access problem. An excellent solution finally came to hand when a local landowner proposed a small part of his property for a parking area. Braesyde now offers a secure place to park, only 12 minutes from the East Face of the Fortress.

The arduous debate over style and climbing ethics is showing signs of settling down. It is now felt that the future is best served by all climbers, from all-bolt sportheads to on-sight diehards, both trying to preserve the rock environment in as natural a condition as possible. That way, climbers can enjoy every aspect of this diverse game, and still leave future generations a legacy that will allow them to find their own challenges.

As the winter snow disappeared from the crags in the spring of 1993 Skaha had emerged as a major development in Canadian rockclimbing. From Howie Richardson's early explorations in 1987 there were now over 260 routes and no end in sight to the potential; access problems were resolved, this first guidebook was published and there was a growing, enthusiastic climbing community in Penticton. Gazing into the crystal bowl of the future, rapid development of new climbs is likely for some time yet, given the acres of unclimbed rock. Climbers will venture more onto the open faces and aretes and start filling in many of the blanks between the climbs of today. Crags untrodden as yet will be opened up, levels of difficulty will rise and thousands of climbers will discover for themselves the magic of Skaha.

Local Facilities

Penticton offers all the resources climbers need. Note that Okanagan Falls, the small community at the south end of Skaha Lake is also a convenient place for groceries and gas for climbers approaching from Washington State.

- ◆ **CAMPING...** Unfortunately there is no recognised Climbers Campground at the present time, although this is sure to change. Meanwhile, try the Okanagan Falls Provincial Campground on Green Lake Rd in Okanagan Falls. The Skaha Beachcomber and Wright's Beach camp, adjacent to each other on highway 97, are also pleasant locations in the northwest corner of Skaha Lake. In addition, there are many large campgrounds which cater primarily to RV's and plenty of quiet backroads.

- ◆ **GROCERIES...** There are a number of large supermarkets in Penticton, the closest of which is in the Cherry Lane Mall at Warren and Main St. There are also several 24hr gas stations which have extensive food bars along Main St and Skaha Lake Road. Good facilities are available too in Okanagan Falls. The closest food store to the crags is South Main Market, 800m north of Crescent Hill Rd.

- ◆ **GASOLINE...** Many 24hr outlets in Penticton.

- ◆ **RESTAURANTS...** Penticton abounds in good restaurants of all kinds. Along Main St between Carmi and Cherry Lane Mall, there are many fast food and pizza shops. Carl's Cafe at 261 Main St is worth stopping at for breakfast. The Spotted Dog, 320 Martin St. (One block west of Main in downtown Penticton) offers a wide variety of good coffees if you need your morning fix.

- ◆ **PUBS...** There are three which are popular with climbers. The Barley Mill on Skaha Lake Road, and Slack Alice's on Lakeside Rd north of downtown Penticton. Both are sizable places and offer food as well as good beer. The Welcome Inn at Gallagher Lake, 12km south of Okanagan Falls, is well worth a visit too.

- ◆ **CLIMBING GEAR...** Ray's Sports Den at 215 Main St (493-1216) in the downtown area of Penticton is the place. Everything you need for the crags, and the best source of local information on new routes and current developments.

- ◆ **SHOWERS...** There are two choices. The Community Pool, north of highway 97 on Power St, a large facility which offers everything from a swim to workouts, showers, saunas and more. Alternatively, the Best Western on Skaha Lake Rd and the Kreekside Motel on Main St both offer a drop-in service for the use of their pool and hot tub.

- ◆ **MOTELS...** There are many motels and hotels of all kinds in Penticton and Okanagan Falls.

- ◆ **INFORMATION SERVICES...** An excellent resource for all kinds of local information is the Tourism Information Service run by the Penticton Chamber of Commerce. (604) 492-4103 or 492-4055.

Some other things to do...

- ◆ BIRDWATCHING... A fine hobby for many in this area, with several species found here and nowhere else in Canada. Try the beach of Okanagan Lake along Lakeside Road and further south at Vaseaux Lake and the north end of Osoyoos Lake.

- ◆ CYCLING - MOUNTAIN BIKING... Excellent trails throughout the region. Ask at The Bike Barn, 300 Westminster for more information. The circuit of Skaha Lake is also popular.

- ◆ THE BEACHES... A great family sunspot at Skaha Beach Park.

- ◆ THE DOMINION ASTROPHYSICAL OBSERVATORY... Tours available of this centre dedicated to study of radio signals from the edge of the universe. Call 497-5788 for more information.

- ◆ BOOKS 'N THINGS... An amazing emporium of good taste in literary stuff opposite the climbing store on Main St.

- ◆ OK FALLS FLEA MARKET... Considered by many to be the capital of the flea-market world. Open almost every day.

- ◆ CINEMA... The Pen-Mar Cinema Centre at 361 Martin St.

- ◆ LOCAL VINEYARDS FOR WINE TASTING TOURS... Call the Tourism Information Service at 492-4103 or 492-4055.

Regional Profile

The City of Penticton lies on a flat plain between Okanagan Lake and Skaha Lake. With a population base of about 29,000 it is the service, administration and trading centre for the southern Okanagan region of British Columbia. Tourism is a major economic generator for the area, with water sports, beaches, golfing, mountain biking, skiing, and now rockclimbing all part of the local economic fabric. Farming, manufacturing and logging also play their part. The hillsides around Penticton are famous for the orchards and vineyards that have made the valley the finest fruit and wine producing area in Canada. The name Penticton is appropriate too; "PEN-TAK-TEN", meaning a place to live forever.

In case of an accident...

Take note that some of the crags are up to 45 minutes walk back to the car, so proceed with caution and invest in first aid training. If an accident should occur and medical assistance is needed, Penticton Regional Hospital provides 24 hour emergency services. The hospital is located at the intersection of Carmi and Industrial Street. If help is urgently needed, phone 911. This will alert the Police who will immediately initiate emergency rescue services.

Wildlife and Conservation

One of the great attractions of the Skaha area is the richness of the plant and animal life which cannot fail to touch everyones' day on the hill. It is especially noteworthy that there are some species which are found nowhere in Canada except the Skaha area. It is therefore important that all climbers show the greatest respect for the creatures and plants who live here. Skaha is their home.

BIRDS... There is a wide variety of species regularly seen here, from large raptors such as bald and golden eagles, hawks, osprey and falcons to the rare canyon wren with its unmistakable descending song. Equally rare is the white throated swift, an agile, noisy flier. The advent of spring is always marked by the cheerful song of the meadowlark proclaiming its territory from a perch and the arrival of mountain and western bluebirds. Sharp eyed climbers may see the common nighthawk and the poorwill hunting at the end of the day and many other interesting species who live in these hills. It goes without saying that nesting areas should be left well alone. Avoid climbs where birds are suspected of nesting.

TREES AND PLANTS... This part of British Columbia is the ponderosa pine - bunchgrass biogeoclimatic zone, better known to the great unwashed as "holiday land". Trees found here include the ponderosa pine which likes the dryer benchlands; douglas fir, more commonly found in the gullies and damper valleys and the occasional stand of lodgepole pine. Among the plants, the characteristic bunchgrass, tall and waving in the wind, is found only on the benches. In early spring, the brilliant yellow flower which covers much of the Okanagan is balsamroot, a sunflower. Among the more spectacular flowers of this time are shooting stars, prickly pears, bitter-root (beautiful pink flowers which grow in bare, rocky ground), mariposa lilies and phlox.

REPTILES AND AMPHIBIANS AND TICKS... Snakes can be found throughout the area, especially in the more open, rocky places. Keep your eyes (and ears) open. Only the western rattlesnake is poisonous, but snakebite incidents have been rare. It is protected, as is the western blue racer, a slim, fast moving snake. Leave well alone. Two lizards are found, the alligator lizard, a lovely slender creature 20-25cm long which is the intermediate host for the ticks; and the western skink, 12-18cm long, noted by its obvious stripes. The tick can be a pest in the early spring and may carry disease. Daily inspection is advised. There are few amphibians, including the spadefoot toad, a protected species.

MAMMALS... Many different common species may be encountered during a day on the hill; black bear, both species of deer, big horn sheep, coyotes, marmots, and of course the wood rat. Of special note are bats, so much so that this is Canada's hot spot for their habitat and study. More species are found here than anywhere else. Rare indeed are the spotted bat and the pallid bat. There have been few encounters by climbers, but be very careful of treading in their terrain. Leave the little critters well alone.

◆ *The information on Wildlife was provided by Howie Richardson.*

Weather and Climate

The weather in this area is a classic continental climate, enjoying hot sunny summers and cool winters, a kind of climbing nirvana where the season typically runs from mid March into mid November. It is rare that a trip to Skaha will be rained out.

Environment Canada has cited the Penticton area as having the best climate in the country, with only 286mm (11") of precipitation per year, lots of sunshine and warm temperatures. When frontal rain is pouring down at Squamish, Skaha invariably offers good climbing conditions. Spring and Fall are the most popular climbing seasons, green and lush in the Spring, and very dry in the Fall. Shade can always be found for climbing in the heat of summer. Frosts can occur early and late in the season. Call (604) 492-6991 for a recorded weather message.

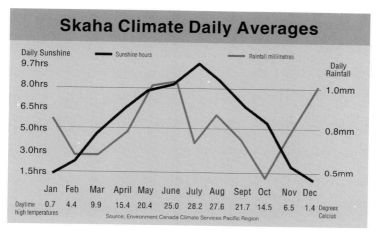

Skaha Climate Daily Averages

Daily Sunshine — Sunshine hours — Rainfall millimetres

	Jan	Feb	Mar	April	May	June	July	Aug	Sept	Oct	Nov	Dec	
Daytime high temperatures	0.7	4.4	9.9	15.4	20.4	25.0	28.2	27.6	21.7	14.5	6.5	1.4	Degrees Celcius

Source: Environment Canada Climate Services Pacific Region

26

Acknowledgements

Many people have contributed toward the publication of this first guide to Skaha; providing obscure information, offering opinion on how best to represent the area and making constructive criticism. I would like to especially thank Robin Barley, Rick Cox, Greg Foweraker, Dean Hart, Dave Jones and Howie Richardson for their enthusiasm and expertise.

Of special note is the role played by Howie Richardson, whose careful notes of route development in the early years and intimate knowledge of the area greatly aided the task of collecting the information. In addition to having made the first ascent of so many climbs, Richardson, who is a biologist, is also an authority on the abundant wildlife in the area, and provided the information for the section on Wildlife and Conservation (and the best pubs).

The opportunity to shoot the aerial photos was kindly provided by Doug Kenyon of Greyback Construction - it made a difference.

Finally, a big thank you to three special people for the support that only a family can give. My wonderful wife Lynn and my sons Barry and Tony. I owe them a lot.

My thanks to everyone

Danny Ashton
Robin Barley
Rick Cox
Hugh and Gail Dunlop
Lindsay Eltis
Greg Foweraker
Rob Greno -
  Penticton Economic
  Development Officer

Dean Hart
Dave Hetherington
Sig Isaac
Dave Jones
Nick Jones
Josh Korman
Ray Keetch
Doug Kenyon

Hugh Lenney
Bert Marchand
Lynn McLane
Anders Ourom
Finbar O'Sullivan
Howie Richardson
Nita Richardson
Les Wiles
Gary Wolkoff

About this book...

This book was created on a 386/33 computer with considerably more memory than the author. The photographs were shot with Nikon equipment onto Fujichrome then scanned onto compact disc with the Kodak Photo-CD. Image files were then edited in Aldus Photostyler, and topo overlays added with Coreldraw, which was also used for mapping and other graphics. Lotus Amipro was used for the manuscript, and also for page layout, assembly and final output. The resulting files (about 150mb) were output direct to film on a Linotronic 330 typesetter by WYSIWYG Graphics. Colour separations for the cover file were output by Lithotech Canada.

Roadside Cliff

A pleasant 20m crag on Valleyview Road, as close to your car as you're ever likely to get. The cliff is a popular evening destination in the summertime heat, steep and fingery with a dozen climbs and variations packed into its 70m length. Climbers have been active here for at least 20 years. There is some bouldering at the base and a trail to the top starts from the south end. The most obvious feature is the right facing, arching corner of *Another Roadside Attraction*. Climbs are described from the left.

❏ **Approach...** From the southern end of South Main Street in Penticton, opposite Lee Ave, turn eastwards up Crescent Hill Rd. Follow it for 0.5km to a junction with Valleyview Rd. Continue south for 1.1km to the crag, behind a screen of trees on the left.

❏ **Parking...** This is a sensitive residential area, so please keep noise to a minimum, and park on the wide shoulder opposite.

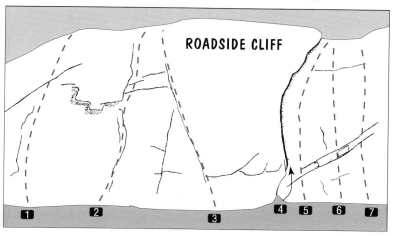

ROADSIDE CLIFF

1   **Swami's Pair-a-dice** 5.11b TR   **28**   15m
    FA: unknown

A face climb 5m to the left of the band of square cut roofs, up a line of rightward facing edges.

2   **Dan's Dream** 5.10a   *   **28** F   20m
    FA: unknown

Just right of the band of roofs, climb an obvious line of flakes leading up to a horizontal fault. Continue up a crack to finish.

28

3 **Leanie Meanie** 5.10b * `28` N 20m
FA: unknown (c. 1990?)

The prominent left leaning hand and fist crack which turns abruptly into fingery face climbing higher up.

4 **Another Roadside Attraction** 5.9 * `28` N 20m
FA: H.Richardson R.Mounsey 1974 [OS]

The most obvious feature on the cliff is this right facing corner in the centre of the crag, leading up to an arching finish.

5 **Steal Your Face** 5.10d TR * `28` 20m
FA: unknown

A steep face climb just right of the corner. Finish at its top.

6 **Iga Uga Chaga Dub** 5.11c * `28` F 20m
FA: unknown

A thin bolted face climb.

7 **Ardent** 5.11b TR * `28` 20m
FA: unknown

Just right of *Iga Uga...* move up to a diagonal fault, then small edges lead to a horizontal crack. Finish up obvious side holds.

8 **Rat-trap** 5.8 N 15m
FA: unknown

An obvious hand sized crack leading up to an alcove below a roof at the right side of the crag. Turn the roof on the left.

9 **The Big Itch** 5.5 N 8m
FA: unknown

A short corner at the far right of the cliff sporting a wide crack and sometimes poison ivy.

Foreplay

This west facing cliff is at the north western edge of the main climbing area, close to Hydro Road. The climbs lie at the southern end of the cliff, and are described from the right.

❏ **Approach...**   From the **Juniper Road parking area,** follow Hydro Road as far as the left turn for Chatsworth. Continue for another 100m to a long crag which can be seen 50m behind the trees on the left. Approach at the south end.

10 **Sunset Boulevard** 5.10d * `30` M 20m
FA: G.Wolkoff R.Cox June 12 1991

Start at the south end of the wall at the toe of a rounded buttress. Follow indistinct cracks and seams, trending left at mid height.

11 **Whine and Dyno** 5.11a * **30** F 20m
 FA: G.Wolkoff R.Cox June 12 1991

Sustained face climbing mid way between *Sunset Boulevard* and the corner to the left.

12 **Mother's Day** 5.7 **30** N 18m
 FA: G.Wolkoff S.Chaytor June 1991 [OS]

An obvious steep ramp with a hand crack in the back, approximately 50m north of the south end of the wall.

FOREPLAY

Western Skink

Kids' Cliff

A smooth east facing cliff which offers several good face climbs, all with fixed protection. You'll like this place if you don't own any wire nuts and you think Friends are people you climb with.

❑ **Approach...** From the **Juniper Road parking area**, head south along Hydro Road and take the left turn onto the dirt road (see map) as for Chatsworth and the Skaha Loop Trail. Follow this roadway uphill, ignoring the Loop Trail where it turns to the right. After another 100m the dirt road begins to veer leftward. At this point, pick up a small trail on the right which heads uphill to the top of the crest some 300m ahead. Just before stepping over a large snag across the trail, start trending up rightward to the south, making for the east side of the prominent knoll (the top of Kids' Cliff). Enter the narrow bushy canyon, which is actually the northern extension of Shady Valley, and continue 50m to the first climb. Climbs are described from the right, and the first starts 5m left of a tall, reddish pine tree.

❑ From **Cave Cliff...** See the Cave Cliff section for description.

❑ From **Chatsworth....** It is possible to walk northward along the crest of Valleyview Ridge from Chatsworth to Kids' Cliff.

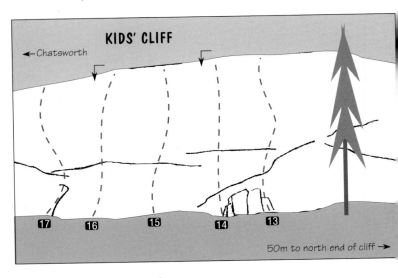

KIDS' CLIFF

←Chatsworth

17 16 15 14 13

50m to north end of cliff →

13 **The Quickening** 5.11a **   **37** F   20m
    FA: N.Jones T.Holwill Oct 12 1992
Start off a block, climb over an arch and up to a horizontal crack. A difficult mantel leads to a handrail. Go back left to finish. 6qd.

14 **Highlander** 5.10d **   **37** F   20m
    FA: T.Holwill N.Jones Oct 12 1992
Very direct and sustained in the lower half. 7qd.

15 **'S Cool Wall** 5.10b *   **37** F   20m
    FA: D.Hetherington H.Richardson June 16 1992 [OS]
Straight up with a jog to the right. Crux near the top. 7qd.

16 **Generation Gap** 5.10a **   **37** F   20m
    FA: H.Richardson T.Richardson R.Mounsey April 1991
Straight up. Crux at the undercling below mid height. 6qd.

17 **Rejuvenation** 5.9 *   **37** F   20m
    FA: H.Richardson D.Hetherington D.Kenyon May 16 1992
Climb a vague groove to a fingery traverse leading leftward and then straight up. 5qd.

Cave Hill

The Cave Hill is one of the more prominent features in the area, and can easily be seen from highway 97, sporting cliffs on three sides. It has long been known to local residents for the unusual and hugely entertaining descent it offers inside the hill, a scramble down a cave system which emerges through a small squeeze hole at the base of the west face. All kinds of people both old and young have descended this cave. In places it is fourth class. Be sure to look for the "Photocopier", a horizontal slot at shoulder height just inside the top entrance. Mail yourself down the wild ride inside, rejoining the main descent lower down. Don't forget to take flashlights!

❏ **Approach for the Cave Hill Descent...** The top of the hill is most conveniently reached by scrambling up from the first break north of the climbs on the east face. Start from the big cleft at the top of the hill and find your own way down. A good alternative to maximise the fun is to climb either of the prominent chimney /gullies just to the west of the climbs on the south face. Follow over and under boulders to the big cleft at the top.

❏ **Approach...** See the **Skaha Loop Trail** description.

32

❏ **From Kids' Cliff...** This approach is the fastest route from the Juniper Road parking area. When on the trail to Kids' Cliff, instead of turning off to the right into Shady Valley and the base of the cliff, continue heading south-east along the trail up the hillside, which becomes more open after 150m or so. The trail climbs gently, turning southward into increasingly dense timber, eventually beginning a gradual descent into a narrow gully, avoiding a series of low rock walls along the way. The South Face of Cave Hill is reached after about 10 - 15 minutes.

Cave Hill West Face

Despite the size of this face, there is only one climb here, the quality of which can be deduced from its name.

❏ **Approach...** See the **Skaha Loop Trail** description for the approach to Chatsworth. Drop down into Shady Valley at the north end of Chatsworth Edge and traverse along to the base. Alternatively, walk around from the base of the South Face.

| 18 | **Bear Shit on a Doorknob** 5.7 | | N | 3p |

FA: H.Richardson F.Metcalf Oct 18 1988 [OS]

An obvious chimney on the west face. Exit left under a loose roof.

Cave Hill South Face

A very prominent, slabby wall offering several moderate climbs on the right side. The climbs are described from the right.

| 19 | **No Sweat Arete** 5.5 | **34** | N | 40m |

FA: R.Mounsey (solo) Sept 26 1992 [OS]

The prominent arete at the corner of the south and east faces.

| 20 | **A Day Out with the Boys** 5.6 | **34** | N | 40m |

FA: H.Richardson Sept 24 1988 [OS]

The big crack and groove line. Step left onto the slab to finish.

| 21 | **Scourge of the Working Class** 5.9 * | **34** | F | 25m |

FA: H.Richardson G.Brace J.Miller Oct 3 1992

Start 10m left of *A Day out with the Boys*. Face climbing leads over 3 gentle slabby overlaps to gain a comfortable ledge and rappel station. 4qd.

| 22 | **Tax Burden** 5.8 * | **34** | F | 40m |

FA: H.Richardson G.Brace Oct 3 1992

A few metres left of *Scourge...*, slabby face climbing leads to the left of the summit. 4qd.

CAVE HILL - SOUTH FACE

to Chatsworth

Cave Hill East Face

The next two climbs are around the corner to the right from *No Sweat Arete*, on the East Face.

23 **Australopithocus** 5.10a * **34** M 25m
FA: D.Hetherington H.Richardson Oct 10 1992
15m right of *No Sweat..* is a short overhanging yellow corner. Begin at its right edge and follows the stepped groove above.

24 **Memories of Des** 5.10b * **34** M 25m
FA: H.Richardson D.Hetherington Oct 10 1992
Another stepped groove 5m right of the previous climb. A broddling stick can help clip a low protection bolt for those who need it. Awkward moves gain the groove, then easier above.

Stove Cliff

A modest little cliff 100m east of Cave Hill.

❏ **Approach...** See the **Skaha Loop Trail** description.

25 **Primus** 5.7 **35** N 20m
FA: H.Richardson B.Cuthbert April 1987 [OS]
The obvious left facing corner in the middle of the crag.

34

26 Optimus 5.9 * `35` M 18m
   FA: H.Richardson D.Hetherington Oct 10 1992

3m right of *Primus*, face climbing leads up left to a big flake, then a step right leads into a crack. On to the top.

27 Bill's Crack 5.8 * `35` N 15m
   FA: W.Noble Sept 27 1992

A handjam crack on the right side of the cliff beside a pine tree.

STOVE CLIFF
25 26 27

THE FAR SIDE
28 29 30 31 32 33

CAVE HILL

The Loop Trail

to Morning Glory

to Chatsworth

The Far Side

An inviting south facing crag 250m east of Cave Cliff, clearly defined by several chimneys and aretes and a large right facing corner at the right (east) end of the crag.

❏ **Approach...** See the **Skaha Loop Trail** description.

28 **Salters Road** 5.10c *   **35**   N   25m
    FA: K.McLane H.Richardson Oct 12 1992 [OS]
Start 10m right of the undercut west end of the cliff below a shallow left leaning flake / arch. Climb it to the left end then pull up onto the ledge above. Belay or continue more easily to the top.

29 **Rat Warren Chimney** 5.5   **35**   N   12m
    FA: H.Richardson (solo) Oct 1992 [OS]
The one metre wide chimney 12m right of a large corner.

> The next 3 climbs lie in the big corner at the east end.

30 **In the Nick of Time** 5.10b *   **35**   N   18m
    FA: K.McLane H.Richardson Oct 12 1992
Start in the centre of the left wall, soon trending left to gain a steep finger sized crackline.

31 **The Max Ferguson Show** 5.10a *   **35**   F   15m
    FA: K.McLane H.Richardson Oct 12 1992
Climbs the leaning wall just right of centre. Generous holds lead to a crux at the top. 2qd.

32 **Throw Zog Throw** 5.10a ***   **35**   F   20m
    FA: K.Sellers W.Noble T.Holwill N.Jones R.Booth Sept 27 1992
An outstanding climb up the impressive undercut arete on the right of the corner. Much easier than it looks! 5qd.

33 **Rottweiler Farm** 5.10a *   **35**   N   18m
    FA: N.Jones R.Booth T.Holwill W.Noble K.Sellers Sept 27 1992
Around to the right from *Zog...* is a steep broken, flaky corner.

Shortcut Cliff

A small steep cliff with a left lean to it, sporting several cracks.

❏ **Approach...** See the **Skaha Loop Trail** description.

34 **Crack of Brawn** 5.10c *   N   22m
    FA: G.Wolkoff June 8 1991 [OS]
Good jamming up the most obvious diagonal crack.

Chatsworth Edge

One of the most popular cliffs at Skaha, with a charming, open aspect on a terrace above Shady Valley. A good variety of easier climbs characterised by short cracks and corners and a sociable atmosphere, has made Chatsworth very popular with beginners. Climbs are described from the left.

❏ **Approach...**   See the **Skaha Loop Trail** description.

35   Parasitoid 5.9   **37** N   15m
    FA: M.Gardiner H.Richardson March 27 1988 [OS]

A short, left facing flaky corner behind a group of small fir trees at the far left of the cliff. Bold moves over the bulge at the top.

36   Gem Quality 5.6   **   **37** N   18m
    FA: H.Richardson R.Cuthbert Aug 11 1987 [OS]

The left-hand of 2 obvious cracks.

The Loop Trail

CHATSWORTH EDGE

37   **Minor Facet** 5.10b * *Attempted May 25/96* 37 M 18m
     FA: H.Richardson R.Mounsey J.Miller Oct 3 1992
A face climb jammed in between the cracks. Take a #1 Friend.

38   **Diamond in the Rough** 5.7 *★★ 37 N 18m
     FA: H.Richardson D.Hetherington Aug 23 1987 [OS]
The right-hand crack, a little harder than its neighbour.

39   **Red Herring** 5.11a * 37 M 18m
     FA: R.Cox July 1989
A pair of thin offset cracks with a bolt between them. Strenuous.

40   **Fox Shooter** 5.10c * 37 M 22m
     FA: R.Barley N.Barley April 13 1990
Yes indeed, the first bolts at Chatsworth. Just right of *Red Herring* is a short, shallow corner. Climb it to the open face above. Long reaches lead to a horizontal crack, then a hard step right leads to a rising traverse and easier ground.

41 **Shake and Bake** 5.10a * `37` N 15m
    FA: D.Hetherington H.Richardson March 28 1988 [OS]
An obvious crack behind a pine tree. After a fingery start, the crack becomes wider and easier.

42 **Artificial Gem** 5.10b * *Attempt* `37` F 15m
    FA: R.Cox G.Wolkoff July 1989 *may 23/96*
A face climb snaking up the wall past 4 bolts.

43 **Fat Boys (Live Longer)** 5.10c * `38` M 15m
    FA: J.Orava H.Richardson S.Knight April 28 1989 [OS]
The next crack, which twists right then left. Steep, fingery and hard to place protection. Being skinny doesn't help either.

44 **Wrecked All Crack** 5.9 ** *may 27/96* `38` N 12m
    FA: D.Hetherington H.Richardson May 22 1988 [OS]
A popular crack climb which starts by a large tree.

45 **Pure Jam** 5.7 * `38` N 10m
    FA: H.Richardson May 22 1988 [OS]
A short crack with a small tree at 6m.

> North from here are 3 cracks about 3 - 4m apart.

VALLEYVIEW RIDGE DESCENT INTO SHADY VALLEY

| 46 | **15 Carat** 5.8 ** | **38** N | 12m |

FA: D.Hetherington H.Richardson Aug 23 1987 [OS]

The left-hand crack starts in a corner. Some awkward jamming.

| 47 | **Centre Crack** 5.8 | **38** N | 12m |

FA: D.Hetherington H.Richardson March 2 1988 [OS]

The hand crack in the centre.

| 48 | **Rough Cut** 5.7 ** | **38** N | 12m |

FA: H.Richardson D.Hetherington Aug 23 1987]OS]

The right-hand crack. Good climbing.

| 49 | **Uncut** 5.7 * | **38** N | 10m |

FA: D.Hetherington H.Richardson Aug 23 1987 [OS]

The right facing corner at the north end of the cliff.

Screeching Wall

Shady Valley continues southward from Chatsworth, and becomes a deep canyon as far south as Doctors' Wall. The east facing wall has one section which is particularly impressive, rearing up to a full pitch in height and sharply featured with bulges and roofs. It is easily identified, bounded on its right side by the long crack of *Sewer Rat* and the left side by the corner / groove line of *Orange Bird*. Climbs are described from the right (north).

❏ **Approach...** See the **Skaha Loop Trail** description.

| 50 | **Sewer Rat** 5.9 * | **41** N | 50m |

FA: R.Barley N.Barley M.Petersen June 27 1988 [OS]

Adventurous.The impressive crack on the right, cruxy near the top.

| 51 | **Isis** 5.11d *** | **41** F | 40m |

FA: D.Hart L.Ostrander April 1991

An awesome climb up the centre of the most impressive part of the wall, snaking cunningly upward through bulges and roofs. Start below an obvious flake part way up the wall. Climb past a bolt to reach it. From the top of the flake, step right and climb past bolts to a small horizontal fault below an overlap. A hard move to the right gains the steep corner rising from the left end of the big roof. Continue over stepped overhangs to belay on the right.

| 52 | **Isis in Chains** 5.11c *** | **41** F | 25m |

FA: D.Hart April 1991

An easier variation which ends at the chains before the final corner, avoiding the crux of *Isis*. Rappel off.

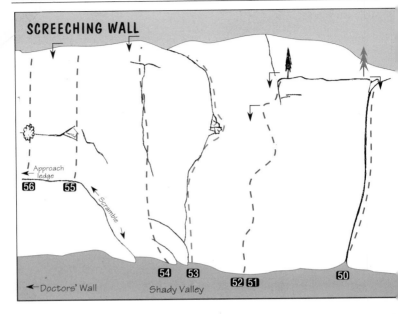

SCREECHING WALL

Approach
ledge
56   **55**

Scramble

← Doctors' Wall   **54**   **53**   **52 51**   **50**

Shady Valley

ISIS

53   **51 52**   **50** →

53 Orange Bird 5.9 * **41** N 40m
FA: R.Barley N.Barley M.Petersen June 27 1988 [OS]

The big right facing corner / groove system easily identified by the orange coloured rock. Excellent climbing degenerates into looser and more vegetated stuff near the top.

54 Flight of the Fledgeling 5.11a ** **41** M 40m
FA: N.Barley R.Barley April 14 1990

Climbs the steep, twisting crack up the wall to the left of the obvious corner of *Orange Bird*. A difficult section leads to a roof. Step left to a thin crack and precarious mantelshelf. Better holds lead to the top.

The next two climbs are side by side, 5m apart at the south end of the Screeching Wall on a short, overhanging wall which rises from a narrow terrace suspended above the floor of Shady Valley. It is well featured with whiteish streaks and enticing rock. Scramble up from the bottom of Shady Valley on the right, or walk in from the Skaha Loop Trail on the left.

55 Hunting Humans 5.11c ** **41** F 18m
FA: D.Hart R.Atkinson

The right-hand route. Very direct face climbing. Steep.

56 Lion's Lair 5.11b * **41** F 18m
FA: R.Atkinson D.Hart

The left-hand route. Climb past a bush, then straight up.

Maternal Wall

Directly opposite Screeching Wall, on the east side of Shady Valley is an equally daunting cliff which also runs from south of Chatsworth Edge to Doctors' Wall. Only one climb has been established to date, opposite *Flight of the Fledgeling*.

❏ **Approach...** As for Screeching Wall on the **Skaha Loop Trail.**

57 My Mother Loves Me 5.11b ** **44** F 35m
FA: G.Edwards R.Paget Aug 1992

A good climb in a fine position. Start below a vague scoop, just south of a pair of tall fir trees. Small open corners and bulges lead to a ledge at 20m. Continue ever upward and begin weaving through larger bulges with good ledges to the top. Many bolts.

The Top Tier

Valleyview Ridge, the escarpment running north - south from Kids' Cliff south to the summit of The Fortress reaches its highest northern point at The Top Tier, sitting high above Doctors' Wall and The Prow. The Top Tier is a small crag with east, south and west faces, and sports several good climbs.

❏ **Approach...**   See the **Skaha Loop Trail** description.

> The next 2 climbs are on the east face.

58   **Mellow Yellow** 5.6   **43** N   10m
　　　FA: H.Richardson (solo) Sept 13 1987 [OS]
A short yellow corner.

59   **Splendiferous** 5.9 **   **43** N   25m
　　　FA: H.Richardson D.Hetherington Aug 23 1987 [OS]
Just right of the big ponderosa pine at the junction of the east and south faces is an incipient crackline running the height of the cliff. Nice climbing on small incuts.

> The next 3 climbs are on the south face.

60   **Peaches** 5.11d **   **43** F   15m
　　　FA: A.Kruger Sept 28 1990
This bolt protected face climb lies on the right of the south face.

61   **Ham Shank** 5.8   **43** N   22m
　　　FA: H.Richardson G.Punnett Oct 10 1987 [OS]
In the middle of the south face are a pair of twisting hand and fist sized cracks. Climb the right-hand. Legs like ham shanks help.

62   **Slacks** 5.9 **   **43** N   18m
　　　FA: H.Richardson D.Hetherington March 28 1988 [OS]
This nice fingery crackline lies at the far left of the face.

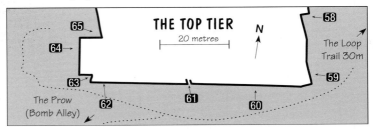

The next 3 climbs lie on the west face, overlooking Skaha Lake, and can be seen from Penticton.

63 Snowbirds 5.7   **43** N   20m
  FA: H.Richardson R.Cuthbert July 11 1987 [OS]
The prominent corner at the junction of the south and west faces.

64 Full Frontal 5.9 *   **43** N   18m
  FA: H.Richardson D.Hetherington March 28 1988 [OS]
The hand crack splitting the wall left of *Snowbirds*. Traverse in from the pedestal on the left.

65 Life in the Slow Lane 5.6   **43** N   18m
  FA: H.Richardson (solo) Sept 13 1987 [OS]
The north facing corner immediately left of *Full Frontal*.

Possible belay

BLIPVERT TOWER

69

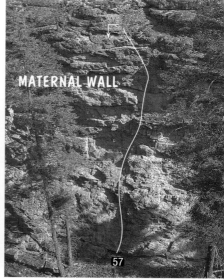

MATERNAL WALL

57

44

Howie Richardson on the first ascent of Max Headroom (Nick Barley)

Grandstand Boulder

South of the Screeching Wall and Maternal Wall on the Skaha Loop Trail, and just before reaching Doctors' Wall, Shady Valley narrows down and is suddenly blocked by a huge pointed boulder, Grandstand Boulder, so called for the fine view it affords of Doctors' Wall. A narrow passage on the east side, Fern Gully, allows easy access to Doctors' Wall and the trails beyond. The next 3 climbs all lie on the Boulder itself.

66 Basement Abortion 5.10a * M 20m
  FA: R.Barley N.Barley May 21 1989
The obvious fingery crackline on the north side. Nice climbing.

67 Easy Does It 5.6 * **50** N 15m
  FA: H.Richardson (solo) June 26 1987
The right-hand of two chimneys in Fern Gully, entertaining.

68 Hexxus the Horrible 5.6 **50** N 15m
  FA: H.Richardson (solo) June 26 1987
The twisting left-hand chimney in Fern Gully.

Blipvert Tower

Immediately north east of Grandstand Boulder is an imposing free standing tower with 2 climbs.

69 Max Headroom 5.10c ** **44** N 30m
  FA: H.Richardson R.Barley (2pa) May 21 1989 [OS]
  FFA: Bruce Kay July 1990 [OS]
Start just north of Fern Gully and climb the corner leading up to a bomb bay slot below the roof. Over the roof and up!

70 Granola Bar 5.9 * **58** F 30m
  FA: G.Hill H.Lenney Sept 1992
A nice face climb up the slabby south side of the tower. At the ledge below the top, keep right for an easy finish

Canyon Wren

Doctors' Wall

This is one of the most popular crags in the area and a good place for an introduction to some of the best routes at Skaha. Doctors' Wall faces east across Shady Gully, and is vertical to overhanging, but well endowed with small holds. The cliff gets the sun until midday, so is a good place for afternoon climbing in the heat of midsummer. Climbs are described from the north.

❑ **Approach...** See the **Skaha Loop Trail** description.
If approaching from Braesyde, under no circumstances approach up Hydro Hill gully, as this will trespass on sensitive private property. Walk around below the East face of the Fortress.

❑ **Descent...** It is worth noting that the scrambling descent from the top of *Doctor Crow* also offers a quick way up to the Top Tier and Valleyview Ridge. At the first decent break left of the main cliff (20m right of Mortician's Slab), scramble up steeply to the big terrace above. Keep right and climb easily up an 8m groove marked by pine trees at its top and bottom. The Top Tier is about 300m to the north across open slopes.

> The next 4 climbs are all gained by scrambling up onto Grandstand Boulder from the south.

71 Squabblers of Skaha 5.10d **   **50** F   35m
FA: N.Barley R.Barley Oct 11 1992
Starting from the north end of Grandstand Boulder, climb up to a pair of shallow left facing corners. Face climb up right over a bulge, then continue direct to finish, arguing all the way.

72 Unethical 5.11a ***   **50** M   30m
FA: N.Barley R.Barley Aug 5 1989
Technical and fingery with awkward protection to start and finish. Face climb up to a line of slim, right leaning ramps. From the top, go left and up a left facing corner to finish. High in the grade.

73 Misdiagnosed 5.11c **   **50** F   35m
FA: L.Eltis Sept 22 1990
A very direct face climb up a rather blank looking wall.

74 Falling into Blackness 5.10d **   **50** M   35m
FA: R.Barley P.Shackleton C.Murrell Oct 27 1991
Step over the crevasse and climb straight up past thin flakes and long reaches to a short, blocky corner. Climb it, then move out right up a flake. Tricky face moves lead up to the final wall.

75 **Extra Billing** 5.10b ** 50 N   30m
   FA: R.Barley N.Henderson H.Richardson Sept 18 1988

Start from the boulders at the base of Grandstand Boulder and climb to an arch. Pull over it on good but widely spaced holds then follow an enticing flake crack to a delicate sting in the tail.

76 **Doctor Megatrip** 5.11d *** 50 F   45m
   FA: L.Ostrander July 1990

A stunning climb offering varied and strenuous climbing. Start just left of *Extra Billing*, and traverse out left along a fault for 10m. (Friends can be useful for protection here). Then weave up the impending wall through bulges and overlaps. Turn the final overhang on the left to a final short slab, where a couple of small wires or TCU's may be useful (if you get there).

77 **PhS** (Piled higher and Steeper) 5.10c *** 49 N   45m
   FA: H.Richardson Aug 18 1988 [OS]

An unmistakable overhanging offwidth crack splitting the wall from top to bottom. Lurch, heave and grovel. Great stuff.

48

Scramble down

82

80

79

81

85

80
79

78

84

82
83
85

81

77

DOCTORS' WALL

Grandstand
Boulder

Fern Gully

78   Grin and Bear it 5.11b **   **49**   F   20m
FA: D.Hart R.Atkinson Oct 30 1990

An excellent climb up the faint crackline left of *PhS*, intersecting with the arch of *The Future is Now*. Start off the left side of the large flake at the base, and climb to belay slings in the overhung arch above. Rappel off or continue up *The Future is Now*.

79   The Future is Now 5.11d ***   **49**   M   40m
FA: D.Hart July 1990

A tremendous climb following the very steep arching overhang above *Grin and Bear it*. Start as for *Malpractice*, climbing the lower corner on good holds. Climb strenuously out rightward under the arch in a superb position, moving left at its end to a memorably devious finish up the headwall above.

> The left end of Doctors' Wall is marked by a high, smooth wall with several excellent face climbs. An easy descent is possible from the ledge above *Doctor Crow* by scrambling down south.

80   Malpractice 5.10d ***   **49**   M   2p
FA: (p1) R.Barley N.Henderson H.Richardson Sept 1988 [OS]
FA: (complete) R.Barley N.Barley B.Protch (1pa) May 20 1989
FFA: R.Atkinson p2 [OS] July1990

A fine climb which shares an initial corner with *The Future is Now*, then breaks out left below the roof to belay on the open wall (5.10a). A hard step left starts the second pitch, followed by lovely steep face climbing (5.10d).

81   Naturopath 5.11b **   **49**   F   40m
FA: G.Wolkoff R.Cox Sept 27 1990

This popular bolted face climb up the wall left of *Malpractice*, provides an alternative form of rock sport to *Doctor Crow*. Climb a short, strenuous bulging wall then move left to climb directly up the steep face above. Small holds but many bolts.

82   Reckless Negligence 5.11a **   **49**   M   2p
FA: N.Barley R.Barley (Alts) Sept 1 1990

A striking line which makes a rising traverse across the wall. Climb through the bulges to the left of *Naturopath* and then make a rising traverse to the belay of *Malpractice* (5.10c). Make a few hard moves up the thin crack above the belay, then swing right to holds in a faint hidden arch. Move right to finish with some awkward moves as for *The Future is Now* (5.11a).

83 **Doctor Crow** 5.10c *** `49` M 40m
    FA: R.Barley N.Barley M.Petersen June 26 1988 [OS]

A Skaha classic. Beautiful crack and face climbing up the centre of the wall. Much easier than its neighbours. The original start was in the corner on the left, but now the *Bolder Start* or *Reckless Negligence* are preferred. The climbing becomes progressively harder above, to a fine finish on the left or the right.

84 **Doctor Crow Bolder Start** 5.10c * `49` N 12m
    FA: H.Richardson M.Gardiner June 24 1988

Start directly below *Doctor Crow* up a short crack, then step right to gain the easier wall above. Bold and poorly protected.

85 **Fingertip Face** 5.10d ** `49` F 35m
    FA: N.Barley R.Barley Oct 6 1990

Good face climbing and a nice crux high up the wall. Take any of the 3 alternative starts to reach big holds below the upper wall of *Doctor Crow*. Trend up left with increasing difficulty to fingery moves over a small roof to gain the headwall. High in the grade.

Mortician's Slab

A small south facing slab 50m left of Doctors' Wall, at the junction of the trails leading to The Fortress and The Prow. Trees offer top-rope anchors above. Scramble up to the ledge at the top on the right, as for the Doctors' Wall descent. Climbs start 4m apart.

❏ **Approach...** See the **Skaha Loop Trail** description.

86 **Down and Dirty** 5.6 `52` N 20m
    FA: H.Richardson R.Cuthbert G.Punnett Aug 11 1987 [OS]

A loose grovel up cracks at the left edge of the slab.

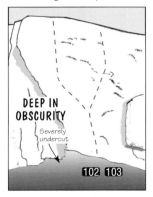

87 **Mr Clean** 5.7   **52**   N   20m

FA: D.Hetherington H.Richardson D.van der Torre Aug 11 1987 [OS]

Climb close to the right edge of the slab. No Protection.

THE PROW

52m

94

93

92

88

89 90

The Prow

A majestic cliff with a fine aspect overlooking Skaha Lake, especially noted for a tremendous line up an enormous blunt arete. The two faces of the Prow, offer slightly different climbing styles. The South Face is a little steeper, especially the upper half, whereas the West Face sports a maze of grooves and overhangs in its lower half, becoming smooth and exposed above.

❏ **Approach...** This cliff is adjacent to private property to the west, and it is essential everyone follows only the two designated access routes to the base.

❏ Do NOT approach from the north along Hydro Road.

❏ Do NOT approach directly from Braesyde via Hydro Hill.

❏ From **Valleyview Ridge...** Leave the Skaha Loop Trail as it descends into the bottom of Shady Valley south of the Screeching Wall, and head up to the Top Tier. From the southwest corner of the cliff, head south, trending rightward until the upper part of the west face of the Prow comes into view. Scramble easily down into Bomb Alley and the base of the west face. 5 minutes or so from the Loop Trail.

❏ From **Doctors' Wall...** Head west past Mortician's Slab. The trail begins to descend, parallel to the rocks on the right, and the Prow soon comes into view. Scramble over the talus to the base. 2-3 minutes from Doctors' Wall.

The Prow South Face

An intimidating wall seamed with steep grooves and bulges, yielding three fine climbs.

88 Slowpitch 5.10c ***   **53** N   2p
    FA: (p1) H.Richardson M.Gardiner May 1988 [OS]
    FA: (p2) H.Richardson R.Barley M.Gardiner June 4 1988

A Skaha classic up the great prow at the corner of the south and west faces. The amazing first pitch up the overhanging lower half of the huge arete is easier than it appears! Start in the groove just right of the toe, and engage in strenuous jamming and bridging up apparently endless grooves and cracks to a fine belay just right of the crest (5.10b). Above the ledge, weave through the bulges following the easiest line. Very exposed. Just below the top, traverse right along a ledge to exit over a slight bulge (5.10c).

54

89   Elysian Fields 5.10c ***   53 N   2p
FA: K.McLane H.Richardson Oct 1989 [OS]

Excellent climbing. Start 10m right of *Slowpitch*, and climb a short wall for about 8m to gain a diagonal crack. Move left along the crack and around an arete to reach the steep ramp on the left. Continue to a large ledge (5.10b). Climb the ramp above, which becomes more exposed. Turn a small bulge on the left, then go up and right to belay at the airy perch shared with *Disparu* (5.10c).

90   Disparu 5.11d ***   53 M   2p
FA: p1 R.Atkinson D.Hart Sept 1992
FA: p2 D.Hart L.Eltis G.Foweraker April 1993

A fine devious climb starting as for *Elysian Fields*. Climb the short wall or broken cracks on the right. Above the diagonal crack, face climbing past bolts leads to the foot of an elegant right facing corner with golden walls. Above the corner, vague bulges lead to a belay in a superb position on a small ledge below the big horizontal fault (5.11c). Traverse right to a bulge then follow steep white grooves and small roofs to the top (5.11d).

91   A Real Piece of Shit 5.10a   N   35m
FA: Z.Caasi H.Yennel Oct 11 1992 [OS]

An awful crack climb disowned by the first ascentionists.

The Prow West Face

A dramatic cliff where some questionable rock adds to the excitement. Climb here for high adventure.

92   Squamish Delight 5.10b **   53 N   2p
FA: R.Cox H.Richardson Oct 1988 [OS]

A steep and audatious line up a long series of grooves. Start 8m left of the toe of The Prow and pull over some blocks to gain a right facing corner groove. Where it forks at 30m, avoid the right-hand flake and continue to a hanging belay on the left (5.10a). Follow the arching overhang above out to the right and step into a big corner which leads to the top (5.10b).

93   Five Tenacious 5.10c **   53 N   3p
FA: R.Barley N.Barley June 1989 [OS]

The centre of the west face is noted by the smooth, blank upper wall. This climb starts 20m uphill from *Slowpitch* beside a large fir tree, at the entrance to Bomb Alley. Just left of a steep broken corner, climb a shallow open groove to a FP on the left at 5m. Above, the groove becomes bigger and more defined. Follow it to a

Rick Cox and Gary Wolkoff on the first ascent of Supercharger (Sue Chaytor)

56

good ledge on the left (5.10b). Step right and climb a good crack which leads back into the main groove to a cave belay on the right (5.9). Up the groove above until a hard move left leads into a higher groove which is followed to the top (5.10c).

94   Bombastic 5.10c *   **53** M   22m
FA: R.Barley N.Barley June 1989

Start 20m up from the fir tree at the bottom of Bomb Alley. Trend slightly right up a steep flaky wall past a bolt to a rest. Face climbing leads to a shallow hole and a skinny pine tree. Climb the short corner above to another fault and belay.

East Portal

This is the large rambling wall on the opposite side of Shady Gully to The Doctors' Wall. It is bounded on its northern end by the tower of Blipvert Buttress and at its southern end by a steep buttress housing the best moderate climb at Skaha.

❑ **Approach...**   This cliff lies inside the Skaha Loop Trail and is easily accessed from the base of Doctors' Wall, or via the trails down from Great White Wall or Sun Valley.

95   Double Exposure 5.8 ***   **58** N   30m
FA: D.Hetherington H.Richardson Feb 28 1988 [OS]

A superb route which is much easier than it appears, following the big cracked ramp striking rightwards across the south face. Start up a subsidiary ramp on the right, soon moving left over a short bulge to gain the main ramp. Follow it with increasing exposure and excitement to an airy belay stance (5.8). Rappel off (50m rope OK), or continue up the direct finish.

96   Double Exposure Direct Finish 5.9 ** **58** N   15m
FA: R.Cox J.Dickie June 1988 [OS]

From the belay at the top of pitch 1, continue up the crack to an awkward step left and final moves to the top. Easier than it looks (5.9). Descend by walking down just south of Go Anywhere Wall.

97   Do the Right Thing 5.10c **   **58** N   35m
FA: D.Hart R.Atkinson May 1990

Start up the ramp just right of *Double Exposure* and follow a steep crackline until difficulties at an overlap force a step left to join the final part of *Double Exposure*. Good climbing.

EAST PORTAL
WEST FACE

101   100

95

Blipvert Tower

70

96

98

101 100

99   95   97

EAST PORTAL
SOUTH VIEW

Great White
Go Anywhere
Ochre Wall

Doctors' Wall
50m

Deep in Obscurity 100m

58

98 Do the Wrong Thing 5.11a *   **58** N   35m
   FA: J.McCallum May 1991

A direct finish to *Do the Right Thing*. Continue straight up the crack to join *Double Exposure* at the belay.

99 A Saner World 5.10c **   **58** M   2p
   FA: R.Barley N.Barley June 25 1990

Climb *Double Exposure* to the bottom of the big ramp, then go left across the white slab on small undercling holds. A better start is to climb the groove on the left to reach the end of the undercling more directly. Continue up past a bolt to an overlap, then left with difficulty to a good ledge belay (5.10c). Swing back right into a large groove, keeping right at the top to avoid loose rock (5.10a).

100 Talking Dirty 5.11a *   **58** M   35m
   FA: R.Cox G.Cox April 1989

This climb is on the west face, directly across from the centre of Doctors' Wall. Climb vegetated ledges to gain an overhanging flake crack leading up to a horizontal break. Step right and finish up an incipient crack on the right side of the gently overhanging wall.

101 Clodhopper 5.9   **58** N   35m
   FA: R.Cox H.Richardson Oct 1988 [OS]

Start left of *Talking Dirty*, then head up the slab to the left, grovelling up a series of dirty cracks and grooves to the top.

Deep in Obscurity

Well named. Shady Valley continues south from Doctors' Wall, becoming very narrow and difficult to navigate. This is a small east facing wall in the gully, about 130m south of East Portal.

❏ **Approach...** 100m south of East Portal and Doctors' Wall on the east side of Shady Valley, drop down into the narrow gully beside a large burnt snag on the ground, and scramble south a few metres to a smooth, undercut, east facing wall 12m high. Two bolted lines share a desperately hard common start. (You have been warned!). The grades apply to the climbing above.

102 Fledgeling 5.11b *   **52** F   12m
   FA: D.Jackson July 1990

Hard boulder moves lead over the undercut. Then follow the left-hand line of bolts to the top.

103 Early Bird 5.11c *   52   F   12m
FA: A.Kruger July 1990

The right-hand line.

> Just before the trail from Doctors' Wall to Go Anywhere Wall enters Sun Valley, the cliffs of East Portal taper into the hillside at a broken buttress. It sports one climb.

104 Forgettable 5.9   N   25m
FA: D.Hetherington H.Richardson Oct 1988

A left leaning crack on the broken buttress leads to a bulge. Onward to the top.

Go Anywhere

An east facing crag in Sun Valley looking across to The Great White Wall which has developed into a popular practise area. As the name suggests, there is an abundance of holds, especially on the slabby face climbs on the right. Access to the top is gained up a gully 50m to the south. Top-roping is convenient and much practised here. Climbs are described from the left.

❏ **Approach...**   From the Doctors' Wall and East Portal area, follow the trail which leads up into Sun Valley and the Great White Wall. The crag is at the trailside. The top of the cliff can be reached easily by hiking up a gully some 50m to the south.

> The first 3 climbs are on the left-hand wall behind the trees.

105 Biceps and Balls 5.9 *   61   M   15m
FA: H.Richardson T.Richardson May 1992

Start just right of the arete at the left edge of the face. Deal with some hardish moves off the ground and also at the final roof.

106 Guts and Bolts 5.10c *   61   M   20m
FA: S.Chaytor G.Wolkoff May 1989

Climb the faint crackline up the centre of the wall. Small wires and technical Friends help.

107 It's About Time 5.9 *   61   M   20m
FA: S.Cox R.Cox Sept 1990

The much bolted face climb on the right of the wall. The difficulty eases higher up.

108 Steve's 5.5   **61** N   20m
FA: S.Knight J.Orava H.Richardson April 28 1989 [OS]
The easy broken corner.

109 Jim's 5.9 *   **61** N   20m
FA: J.Orava H.Richardson S.Knight April 28 1989 [OS]
A good crackline right of the corner.

110 Go Here 5.7   **61** N   22m
FA: S.Chaytor G.Wolkoff May 1989 [OS]
The curious moon shaped flake arch. Start on the left.

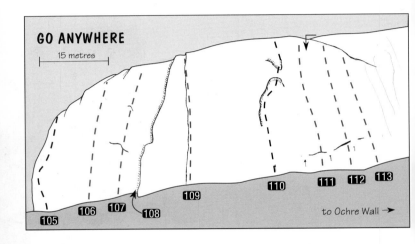

GO ANYWHERE

15 metres

to Ochre Wall →

The next 3 climbs are all good face climbs on the right-hand wall. The rock is slightly suspect in places. Protection is not great, but top-roping is quite convenient.

111 Tony the Tiger 5.8 **   **61** F   20m
FA: H.Richardson T.Richardson May 18 1989
The left-hand face climb. Good.

112 Quo Vadis 5.7 **   **61** F   20m
FA: H.Richardson S.Knight J.Orava April 28 1989
The central face climb. Runout in the easier midsection.

113 Corporate Bladder 5.8 *   **61** F   20m
FA: H.Richardson S.Chaytor May 14 1989
The right-hand climb. Runout to start.

Ochre Wall

Ochre Wall is a steep crag about 100m long facing east across to the north end of the Great White Wall. It is split by several cracklines at its south end. Climbs are described from the left.

❏ **Approach...** 100m north of Go Anywhere, a golden wall comes into view on the left. The cliff beyond is hidden behind the trees.

114 Snakeskin Tracksuit 5.12c *　　　　**62**　F　　20m
FA: D.Jackson Sept 1990

Sustained, well protected climbing on somewhat friable flakes up the gently overhanging golden wall. A tree above the climb can be used for top-roping.

115 Professional Strength 5.11a **　　　**62**　N　　35m
FA: R.Barley H.Richardson N.Barley May 21 1989

The prominent steep crack at the right of the golden wall. Fingery jamming leads to a crux at 10m. Holds on the right wall are useful.

116 Industrial Strength 5.9 **　　　　**62**　N　　35m
FA: H.Richardson D.Hetherington D.van der Torre Oct 11 1987 [OS]

A polished wide crack 10m right of *Professional Strength*.

117 Pin Cushion 5.10d **　　　　　**62**　M　　20m
FA: R.Cox G.Wolkoff May 14 1989

8m right of *Industrial Strength*, this twisting crackline snakes up the wall, finishing just right of a small snag. Good climbing.

118 Men at Work 5.10a *　　　　　**62**　N　　20m
FA: G.Wolkoff R.Cox May 14 1989

The next hand and finger crack. A hard move leads over the bulge.

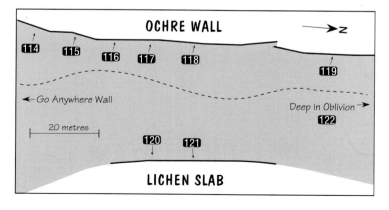

To the right of Men at Work is a ramp which cuts rightward up the cliff. The next climb starts 15m right of the ramp, a steep, vague crackline marked by 3 FP.

119 Skaha Dogs 5.10c *   **62** M   22m
FA: R.Barley H.Richardson May 21 1989
Gently overhanging on good but widely spaced holds. Strenuous.

The Lichen Slab

Directly opposite Ochre Wall is a rather mossy slab with 2 cleaned lines 3 - 5m apart. Climbs are described from the left.

120 Gotta Lichen It 5.9   **62** M   25m
FA: S.Chaytor G.Wolkoff Sept 1989
A direct line up the slab. Start behind a huge, leaning pine tree.

121 Lichen it or Not 5.10a   **62** M   25m
FA: G.Wolkof S.Chaytor Sept 1989
Similar to its neighbour, but a little harder with an awkward mantel onto the headwall.

The next climb is 200m north of Ochre Wall. Follow the footpath northwards to a short wall with a cleaned crack

122 Deep in Oblivion 5.8   N   20m
FA: H.Richardson R.Mounsey Oct 1992 [OS]
Jam the crack into deepest oblivion. No-one will ever know.

Mariposa Lily

Little White Wall

Above Shady Gully on the east side, looking west toward Chatsworth Edge, is a long low outcrop with an idyllic perspective above a wide grassy bench. Despite its 500m length, there are only 4 climbs here. The rock is characterised by numerous tiny holds. The climbs are located close together approximately in the centre of the cliff with *Cornercopia* being an obvious feature.

❏ **Approach...** From north via the Skaha Loop Trail between Cave Hill and Chatsworth Edge, or the south via Go Anywhere Wall.

❏ From **Go Anywhere Wall...** Scramble up a gully at the south end of Go Anywhere Wall ending in a narrow slot which leads up to the benchland above. Head north west up the wide crest, through one more narrow rock band, then start dropping toward Shady Gully, traversing along the hillside. Little White Wall can be seen on the right as a low outcrop.10mins.

❏ From the **Skaha Loop Trail...** The cliff can be reached from the South Face of Cave Hill. Head southwest, dropping down towards Shady Gully to reach the north end of Little White Wall.

123 **Cornercopia** 5.9 * `64` N 15m
FA: D.Hetherington D.van derTorre H.Richardson Oct 11 1987 [OS]
A prominent right facing corner. An obvious feature.

124 **The Rest is Inconsequential** 5.6 `64` N 15m
FA: M.McFadyean H.Richardson Aug 9 1987 [OS]
A wide chimney and jammed block.

125 **Muscles and Testicles** 5.10a * `64` N 15m
FA: H.Richardson Aug 9 1987 [OS]
The left leaning crack. Strenuous to get out of the sentry box.

126 **Brace Yourself** 5.7 `64` N 15m
FA: H.Richardson M.McFadyen R.Cuthbert Aug 9 1987 [OS]
A left facing corner sporting a wide crack behind some bushes.

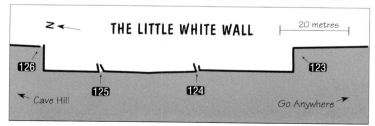

THE LITTLE WHITE WALL — 20 metres

Great White Wall

An exhilarating cliff, magnificently featured by jutting aretes and deep corners which dominates the view of the eastern side of the climbing area. It can be seen clearly from the west side of Skaha Lake. One of the best in the area, it has produced some brilliant climbs. Climbs are described from the left (north).

❏ **Approach...** See the **Skaha Loop Trail** description.

❏ From **Doctors' Wall...** Take the trail leading up past East Portal into Sun Valley. Just as the trail begins to curve to the north before Go Anywhere Wall, another faint trail takes off for the Great White Wall, trending right at first, then more directly toward the crag. Scramble down a short step to the base of the large scree slope below the cliff. Hike up it to the base.

❏ From the **north end of the Fortress...** Drop down into Shady Valley and hike eastward past The Wave to join the Skaha Loop Trail just before Elusive Edge. Continue northward from there.

127 Logan's Run 5.10c *   **66** F   22m
FA: R.Atkinson T.Ryan D.Hart April 19 1992
Start behind the first tree north of *Mrs Palmer*. Trend up left to a vague corner and a bolt. Straight up the broken wall above to a more prominent right facing corner. Climb it, then make a wild exit right to a belay ledge.

128 Mrs. Palmer 5.10a ***   **66** N   2p
FA: H.Richardson D.Hetherington Nov 6 1987 [OS]
The big corner/ramp with stepped overhangs and bulges, becoming more difficult higher up (5.10a). Finish leftward across the slab and an overhanging corner (5.8). Excellent climbing.

129 Wings of Desire 5.11b ***   **66** N - F   45m
FA: D.Hart B.McDonald June 1990
This dramatic crackline splitting the wall gives a magnificent climb. Move into the crack from the left and follow it with tenacity. Very steep with occasional rests. Enter the prominent right facing corner above to a good rest below a roof, then pull out leftward to the final exciting moves. The route is usually climbed using only bolts beside the crack, but natural protection is also available.

130 Ankleduster 5.11c **   **66** M - F   25m
FA: D.Hart R.Atkinson May 1991
A good variation on *Wings...* When the angle of the crack relents, step right and face climb up past 3 bolts. Crux at the end.

Descent

Descent

North

Central

Doctors' Wall

Loop Trail

South

GREAT
WHITE
WALL

GREAT WHITE WALL - NORTH

Descent →

Descent

130

131

127

128 129

132   133

131 **Gang Bang** 5.10c *** `66` N 2p
FA: H.Richardson D.Hetherington C.Murrell D.McCashin Sept 5 1987

The big square corner in the centre of the cliff is a dominating feature, and provides an exhilarating climb in a fine situation, good rests and good protection. Strenuous and technical climbing in the lower corner leads to an easier section beyond which is some superb stemming. Take a big rack! (5.10c). A short final pitch leads from the large ledge to the top (5.8).

132 **Dryathlon** 5.8 `68` `66` N 2p
FA: D.Hetherington H.Richardson Aug 30 1987 [OS]

The impressive white wall to the right sports a large ramp at its left side which steepens into a corner and intersects the ledge at the top of *Gang Bang* (5.8). Climb the short final pitch of *Gang Bang* to the top (5.8).

133 **Acid Test** 5.12a *** `68` `66` M 35m
FA: J.McCallum Sept 1990

A faint crackline cuts diagonally up the lower right-hand part of the formidable white wall right of *Gang Bang*, a real tour de force. Pull up onto an easy slab to reach a shallow, stepped corner. Hard climbing along the crack and face, physically and technically demanding, leads to a junction with *Test of the Ironman*. Continue up *Test...* with whatever strength you have left.

134 **Test of the Ironman** 5.11c *** `68` M 2p
FA: R.Barley N.Barley P.Shackleton (2pa) April 16 1990
FFA: Uncertain May 19 1990

A large blunt arete marks the right-hand edge of the impressive white wall giving one of the mightiest climbs at Skaha. Start up a small flying buttress which gives easy access to the base of the arete. Step up to the right, then head up left into a system of shallow corners weaving through the bulges into a steep groove. Protection is mostly fixed. Easier climbing above leads to a ledge belay (5.11c). Move left and continue straight up to finish (5.10c).

135 **Flying Yorkshireman** 5.10d ** `68` M 2p
FA: R.Barley N.Barley June 1989 [OS]

A lesser companion to *Ironman...*, but nonetheless a good climb. Start up the same flying buttress, then make a rising traverse across the wall to the right following a prominent, sustained crackline. A small overhang provides a tricky step to the right to gain the corner of *Fun Run*. Belay in the corner above (5.10d). Heave up over a cute bulge and on to the top (5.10a).

136 **Fun Run** 5.10a ** 68 N 2p
FA: H.Richardson D.Hetherington March 13 1988 [OS]

To the right of *Ironman...* the left-hand of two corners gives a nice climb. Belay in the corner below the top bulge (5.10a). Steep moves around a bulge give a rather exciting finish (5.9).

137 **Eyrily Hanging Out** 5.11a *** 68 M 2p
FA: P.Shackleton R.Barley N.Barley R.Shackleton Sept 2 1990 [OS]

An intimidating, exciting climb through stepped, arching roofs. Follow the corner crack up to the roof, then pull through to a fine perch (5.10c). Ravens are known to nest here occasionally. Ferocious underclinging above gives a fine exposed finish (5.11a).

138 **The Painted Bird** 5.11d ** 69 F 25m
FA: (TR) L.Ostrander July 1990 FA (1pa): T.Gwynn 1991
FFA: unknown Oct 1992

Start behind a big fir tree, 10m north of the corner of *Horseshoes..* Climb easily up steep, stepped ledges heading for a band of roofs, Above a left facing corner, continue another 5m to a sling belay.

GREAT WHITE WALL
CENTRAL

132   133   134 135   136   137

68

139 Horseshoes, Handtraverses and Hoffwidths 5.11a *** **69** M 2p
FA: (p1) H.Richardson N.Henderson R.Barley (1pa) Oct 1988
FA: (p2) R.Barley N.Barley June 26 1990 FFA: (p1) R.Cox June 1989

A tremendous climb up an impressive right leaning corner capped by a very large roof. Climb the corner with occasional forays onto the right wall to a strenuous position at its top. Hand traverse wildly left to a belay perch, #3-3½ Friend useful (5.10d). Step left, then difficult moves lead up across the exposed face to a hand crack and a rest. Climb the final, easier offwidth crack (5.11a). The first pitch stays dry even in heavy rain.

140 Thundercling 5.10b * **69** F 35m
FA: N.Barley R.Barley June 27 1990

A climb which weaves a diagonal line up the wall just right of *Horseshoes...* Start 5m right of the corner up an obvious steep ramp leading up into the middle of the wall.

GREAT WHITE WALL - SOUTH

The next 5 climbs are on the orange coloured, south facing wall above the benchland at the south of Great White. Scramble up onto the terrace below the climbs, from the right (east). This terrace is not called Rattlesnake Ledge for nothing.

141 **Bull Corner** 5.6 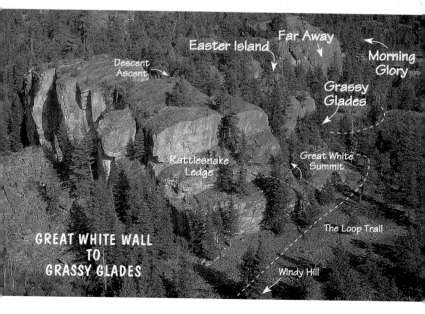 69 N 10m
FA: H.Richardson (solo) Aug 5 1988 [OS]
Dirty, but easy enough to compensate for that.

142 **Crotalus Crack** 5.9 ** 69 N 15m
FA: H.Richardson D.Hetherington Aug 5 1988 [OS]
A good finger crack just left of the corner.

143 **Amazing Grace** 5.10c ** 69 F 15m
FA: D.Hart R.Atkinson April 19 1992
A good face climb 5m left of *Crotalus Crack.*

144 **Venomous** 5.10d ** 69 M 18m
FA: N.Barley R.Barley June 30 1991
Left of the centre of this face, climb a thin crack leading up to a small left facing corner. Finish directly above.

145 **The Tribes of the Unwashed** 5.10c ** 69 M 18m
FA: K.McLane C.Murrell April 4 1993 [OS]
An exciting, exposed climb up the left edge of the face. Start as for *Venomous*, then traverse left past a FP to reach a crack in the arete. Swing into the crack then up steeply on good holds .

GREAT WHITE WALL
TO
GRASSY GLADES

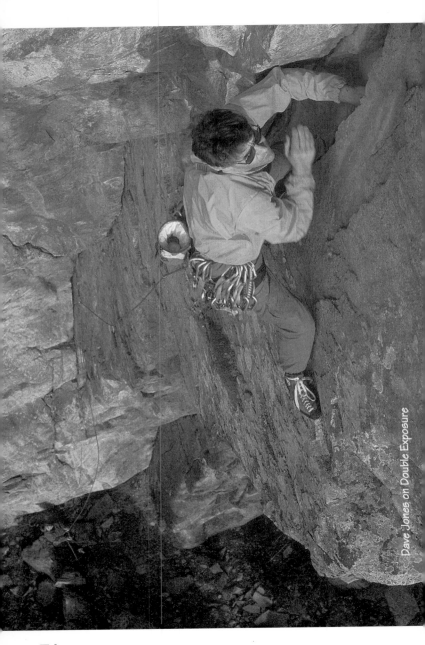

Dave Jones on Double Exposure

East of Great White Wall, the landscape is made up of beautiful grassy benches which lead northward to Morning Glory There are 3 cliffs in this area with climbs.

Grassy Glades

An east facing cliff 150m from the south end of Great White Wall. with one very obvious crack.

146 Grassy Glades 5.10a ***   N   30m
FA: R.Barley N.Henderson Sept 20 1988
An excellent climb up the appealing hand crack.

Easter Island

This is a sheltered, east facing cliff in the first wide gully running north-south, northeast of Grassy Glades, offering several good climbs. Descend northwards down a ramp or by rappeling.

147 Sinners in Paradise 5.5   72 N   35m
FA: D.Jones P.Oxtoby April 12 1993
A prominent fingers to hand size crack in a corner on a south facing wall 50m north of *Grassy Glades*. Tree belay or walk off.

For the main cliff of Easter Island, walk north 80m into an open gully with an obvious cleaned wall on the left The next four climbs start beside or right of a log which butts into the cliff.

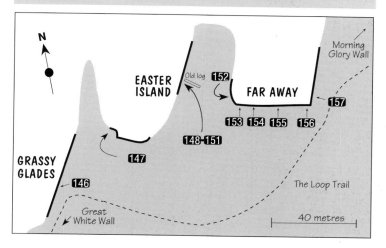

148 **Jumpin' for Jesus** 5.10a **   **72**   M   20m
FA: P.Oxtoby D.Jones April 12 1993

2m left of the log, step up right into a face crack just left of the first prominent corner. Climb the crack into the corner and over the roof above a bolt. Continue on good holds. Bolt belay.

149 **Black Mass** 5.10b **   **72**   M   20m
FA: D.Jones P.Oxtoby April 12 1993

The lefthand of 2 prominent corners, just right of *Jumpin' for Jesus*. Climb the corner and over the roof on large jugs past a bolt.

150 **Satanic Verses** 5.10a **   **72**   M   20m
FA: D.Jones P.Oxtoby April 12 1993

The right-hand prominent corner 10m right of the log. Up and around small corners until able to stem the main corner to the roof. Over the roof on large jugs past a bolt to the belay.

151 **Blood on the Tracks** 5.10a *   **72**   N   25m
FA: P.Oxtoby D.Jones April 12 1993

The last obvious crack at the north end of the wall, broken near the top by the access ledge.

Far Away

150m northeast of Grassy Glades and just east of the gully containing Easter Island is a high, prominent south facing slab with an arete at its right side and a very steep east face. Descend by walking off to the north or by rappel. Climbs are described from the left (west).

152 **Tunnel of Love** 5.6   **72**   N   15m
FA: P.Oxtoby (solo) April 11 1993

An obvious, low angle narrow chimney across from Easter Island, the most southerly feature on the west facing wall, 10m right of a small cave. Requires wide pro.

153 **Big White Dogma** 5.5   **72**   N   25m
FA: P.Oxtoby (solo) April 10 1993

The leftmost and larger of 2 obvious left facing white corners on the south face. Climb the slab then right into the corner.

154 **Rose in the Corner** 5.7   **72**   N   30m
FA: P.Oxtoby (solo) April 13 1993

The right-hand white corner on the south face. Climb the slab then go right into the corner.

155 Revolution Tea Party 5.8   **72** M   35m
FA: P.Oxtoby D.Jones April12 1993

4 metres left of *Anarchist's Arete* is a prominent tree on the south face. Climb up to it via a broken corner, then go right onto the slab and continue directly up past bolts.

156 Anarchist's Arete 5.10b *   **72** M   35m
FA: P.Oxtoby D.Jones April 4 1993

Start at the right-hand end of the south face, and pull steeply up past a FP to gain the slabby wall. Traverse right below a small overhang and continue up the right-hand edge of the face.

157 Question Authority 5.10a **   **72** N   35m
FA: D.Jones P.Oxtoby April 4 1994

Start 10m right of the toe of the arete. Climb into an overhanging alcove, then move right to gain a long, cracked ramp. The ramp is much easier than the climbing below.

Morning Glory

This is the most easterly of the cliffs in this guide, a long, spectacular wall facing east across the Grand Canyon to more cliffs still unexplored. It is especially charming in the early morning, but also offers an escape from the heat in the afternoon. The climbs all start from a narrow terrace below the cliff and are described from the south.

❏ **Approach...** See the **Skaha Loop Trail** description.

158 Flying Flowers 5.9 **   **75** N   35m
FA: G.Wolkoff S.Chaytor May 1989 [OS]

An obvious hand and finger sized crackline which passes through a small alcove at 18m.

159 Squeezy Stomach 5.6 *   **75** N   35m
FA: S.Chaytor G.Wolkoff May 1989 [OS]

A prominent, twisting chimney which is clearly visible from the benches to the south east.

160 Hidden Corner 5.6 **   **75** N   35m
FA: S.Chaytor G.Wolkoff May 1989 [OS]

An impressive climb which takes the huge chimney gully 10m right of *Squeezy Stomach*. Start on the right and climb up left into the chimney along a broken crack. Move up the chimney and step right onto a ledge and up to an alcove. Climb the hidden corner on the right wall which is followed to the top.

MORNING GLORY

158 159 160

The Loop Trail

← Great White Wall

161 Supercharger 5.10d ***   **76** N   40m
FA: R.Cox G.Wolkoff May 1989
50m right of *Hidden Corner* is a superb left facing corner which leads up to a roof and a crack splitting the headwall above. Jump up to gain the first jugs. No cheating stones, but shoulder stands are cool. High in the grade!

162 Rock up Another One 5.7   **76** N   18m
FA: S.Chaytor G.Wolkoff May 1989 [OS]
A short easy corner to the right which starts above ledges.

163 Black Acid 5.10a **   **76** M   25m
FA: R.Cox G.Wolkoff May 1989
A face climb up the golden coloured wall just right of *Rock up Another One*. Follow the black streaks past several bolts.

161

162

163

The Loop Trail

Northern end of Morning Glory 100m →

The Far Side 300m →

Meadowlark

The Fortress

Dominating the southern landscape of the climbing area is a majestic domed hill with a complex series of cliffs on almost every side. This is the Fortress. Many of the climbs are among the best and most popular at Skaha. A hike to the top of the Fortress, a pleasant side trip off the Skaha Loop Trail affords excellent views of the whole area, as well as Skaha Lake and the surrounding hills.

The Fortress is actually comprised of several climbing areas, each with its own character and approach. The great majority of climbs are found on two big cliffs along Shady Valley, both facing away from Skaha Lake. The most popular, at the southern end of the Fortress is the **East Face**, offering many climbs in the 5.10 - 5.11 range. At the northern end, **Red Tail Wall,** named after the Red Tail Hawks which frequent the area, stands high above Shady Valley, its great sweeps of granite breached by several superb climbs, also in the same range of difficulty.

The cliffs on the Fortress are described in a clockwise direction, starting with several climbs near the summit.

❏ **Approaches...** Red Tail Wall, Another Buttress, the Corridor Wall, and the East Face, all lie on the Skaha Loop Trail. See the Loop Trail description and map for details. The South Face has only one climb, best approached from the south end of the East Face. There is one climb at present on the western side of the Fortress. Due to private property to the north, this can be approached only via the trail from the Braesyde parking area. The Turret and Nacho Wall are found near the summit of the Fortress, and can be approached from several directions, most easily by leaving the Loop Trail at the point where it meets the first rocks at the north end of the Fortress. See the Skaha Loop Trail description and map.

The Turret

This cliff is near the summit of the Fortress and offers four climbs, including one of the best 5.9's at Skaha. Superb views in all directions. Climbs are described from the right.

Approach... From **the north:** At the point where the Skaha Loop Trail meets the first rocks at the north end of The Fortress, scramble up a short step on the right and continue up the open hillside heading for the summit area. A small buttress on the ridge crest marks a fork. Below the rocks, go left along a ledge for Red Tail Wall, otherwise move right past the small buttress and continue up the hill. Just before reaching the summit, go left down a narrowing ramp. This soon gives way to a sloping grassy bench below Nacho Wall, a steep wall featured with crispy golden holds. To reach The Turret, continue down the bench staying close to the rock. A short rise leads to the cliff, overlooking a wide bench.

THE FORTRESS AREA

The Turret

168 Nacho Wall

167 166 165 164

The Prow

The Fortress

Doctors' Wall

Red Tail Wall

The Turret

Windy Hill

Shady Valley

East Face

The Loop Trail

Peach Arete

Red Tail Hawk

164 **Gritstoned** 5.10c *   **78** N   15m
     FA: R.Barley N.Barley Oct 11 1992
Just right of the large tree, climb a slanting crack. Easier above.

165 **The Dream** 5.9 ***   **78** N   18m
     FA: H.Richardson D.Hetherington Oct 15 1988 [OS]
Beautiful well protected climbing up a corner and roof system. Easier than it looks.

166 **Abrasive Reality** 5.10a **   **78** M   18m
     FA: N.Barley R.Barley April 1990
The blunt arete gives a technical and exciting climb.

167 **The Bones** 5.6 *   **78** N   15m
     FA: H.Richardson Oct 15 1988 [OS]
The crack on the south face.

Nacho Wall

This is an east facing cliff immediately below the summit, just west of the Turret.

❏ **Approach...** See the approach for the Turret.

168 **Cheese Nacho Wall** 5.10d * **78** F 18m
FA: R.Barley N.Barley Oct 11 1992
A well protected face climb on curious holds. Rappel off.

Red Tail Wall

This is the high, impressive, northern wall of the Fortress, facing east across to the benches of Windy Hill. Despite the extent of the cliff, climbs established to date are all concentrated at the northern end, which is split by an exposed slanting fault, Dead Hawk Rake, which can be walked from end to end, effectively creating the Lower Tier. The climbs are concentrated on the immaculate wall at the right side of the cliff above Dead Hawk Rake. Climbs are described from the right (north).

❏ **Approach...** See the **Skaha Loop Trail** description.

169 **Assholes of August** 5.10a *** **82** N 35m
FA: H.Richardson N.Barley R.Barley Aug 1988
The beautiful crackline at the right side of the face. Pull over a bulge to get started. Easier but sustained thereafter.

170 **Treasure in the Lichen** 5.11a *** **82** F 40m
FA: H.Lenney Sept 1992
Start 4m left of *Assholes...* Climb through initial bulges on good holds then follow a long, elegant line of edges directly up the cliff.

171 **H** 5.11c *** **82** F 45m
FA: H.Lenney Oct 3 1992
Climb into a right facing groove and exit to a short crack above. Exposed face climbing above is punctuated by good rests.

172 **Tierdrops** 5.11d *** **82** F 45m
FA: H.Lenney Sept 1992
Start 5m left of *H*. Pull over two bulges separated by a short wall. Continue in a direct line to the top. Sustained.

173 **Diamond on the Roof** 5.11d ** **82** F 45m
FA: H.Lenney Oct 11 1992
Start behind a large pine tree. A bolt can be clipped from below with a long broddling stick. Otherwise, small wires and a Friend may suffice. Gain the overhung alcove from the left. Pull through the next bulge to gain the main wall and an obvious chipped hold. Superb face climbing leads very directly to the top.

80

174 Three Guys in a Girdle 5.10c * `82` M 3p
FA: H.Lenney M.Gardiner D.Glendenning Oct 10 1992

An intriguing climb, the only girdle traverse at Skaha. Pull over the initial bulge of *Assholes of August*, then trend up leftward to *Treasure in the Lichen*. Move left to join *Tierdrops*. Climb down (back-rope protection off bolts) until above the lip of the roofs below, and go left to join *Diamond on...* and belay (5.10c). Make a rising traverse up to the left for about 15m to a fault which rises diagonally up the wall. Belay just before joining *Dirty with the Money* (5.10a). A short pitch then leads to the top (5.8).

> A 5.11d TR problem exists off bolts on Three Guys in a Girdle. Start at H and climb rightward up through the bulges.

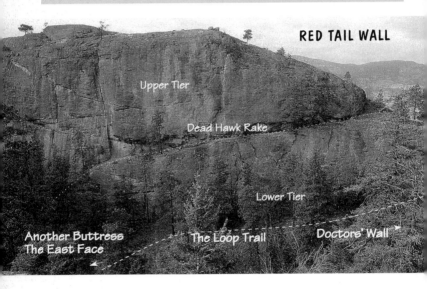

RED TAIL WALL

Upper Tier

Dead Hawk Rake

Lower Tier

Another Buttress
The East Face

The Loop Trail

Doctors' Wall

175 Dirty with the Money 5.8 `82` N 50m
FA: H.Richardson D.van der Torre June 19 1988 [OS]

40m to the left of *Assholes...* and 30m up from the bottom of Dead Hawk Rake, the wall is split by this long corner / crack.

> At the bottom of Dead Hawk Rake are 2 climbs 2m apart.

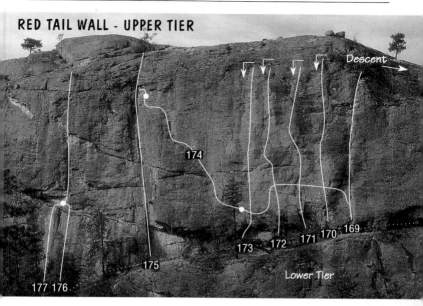

RED TAIL WALL - UPPER TIER

Descent

174

173 172 171 170 169

175

Lower Tier

177 176

Upper Tier

169

178

179

180

182 181

Doctors' Wall

183

The Loop Trail

RED TAIL WALL - LOWER TIER

Robin Shackleton on Falling into Blackness (Robin Barley)

176 Conductress on the Number 19 5.10a (2pa) ** **82** N   2p
FA: H.Richardson D.Hetherington C.Murrell (2pa) [OS] May 22 1988

A major crack and chimney line offering excellent climbing. Some minor aid was used on the first ascent.

177 Bolter Dan 5.9 **   **82** M   25m
FA: unknown (c.1990)

An appealing line up thin cracks and edges.

Red Tail Wall - Lower Tier

The climbs on the Lower Tier below Dead Hawk Rake are pitched at an accommodating angle. Most of them can be top-roped. Climbs are described from the right (north). Note the big pine tree on Dead Hawk Rake above *The Risk is All*, a useful reference.

❏ **Approach...** See the **Skaha Loop Trail** description.

178 Thinbar 5.8 *   **82** N   25m
FA: H.Richardson F.O'Sullivan D.Kenyon April 2 1992

Start 18m right of *The Risk is All*. Climb to a horizontal fault at 7m. Pull over an overlap into a thin left leaning crack which peters out into face climbing.

179 Spring Fingers 5.8 ** Lead Oct 11/96 **82** F   30m
FA: H.Richardson F.O'Sullivan April 2 1992

A good, direct face climb, 10m right of *The Risk is All*.

180 The Risk is All 5.7   **82** N   30m
FA: H.Richardson Oct 5 1992 (solo)

The big pine tree on Dead Hawk Rake marks the top of this sparsely protected face climb. The difficulties are in the last 10m.

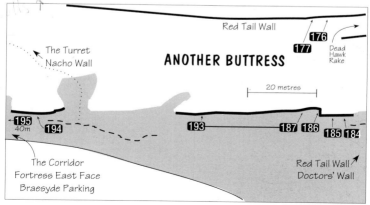

Red Tail Wall

The Turret
Nacho Wall

ANOTHER BUTTRESS

176
177
Dead Hawk Rake

20 metres

195
40m
194

193

187 **186** **185** **184**

The Corridor
Fortress East Face
Braesyde Parking

Red Tail Wall
Doctors' Wall

The next two climbs start close together and climb up
to Assholes of August on the Upper Tier.

181 The Idles of March 5.8 **   82 F   20m
    FA: H.Richardson A.Todd A.Todd March 26 1992
Good climbing. Mantel up onto a big foothold on the right (5.9!).
Generous holds lead to a bolt, then trend up left to the top.

182 Preface 5.10a *   82 F   26m
    FA: H.Lenney G.Hill Sept 1992
A nice face climb. Start 3m left of *The Idles...*

183 Different Reality 5.10a   82 M   28m
    FA: D.Hetherington L.McLane H.Richardson Oct 11 1992
Start below a large pine tree on Dead Hawk Rake, 20m left of
Preface. Climb over a small overlap, trend up right to finish.

Another Buttress

A rather nondescript wall in the bed of Shady Gully just south of
and below the Lower Tier, giving several moderate but entertaining
climbs. The most obvious feature is the left facing corner of *Be
Happy*. Climbs are described from the right.

❏ **Approach...** See the **Skaha Loop Trail** description.

184 Gollum 5.7   84 N   18m
    FA: unknown
The right-hand of two cracklines immediately right of *Be Happy*.

185 Bilbo Baggins 5.8   84 N   18m
    FA: unknown
The left-hand crack.

186 Be Happy 5.6 *   84 N   20m
    FA: G.Wolkoff S.Chaytor Aug 1989
The obvious left facing corner. A pleasant stroll.

187 Don't Worry 5.6 **   84 N   20m
    FA: S.Chaytor G.Wolkoff Aug 1989
The crack immediately left of the corner. Just as pleasant.

188 Lichen in My Panties 5.8 **   84 F   22m
    FA: G.Hill H.Lenney Sept 1992
An excellent face climb on good holds, 3m left of the corner. 5 qd.

FORTRESS EAST FACE - NORTH

Descent

203
202
201
200
199
198
197
196
195

e it in Her Panties 5.8 *   `84` F   22m
  FA: H.Richardson K.McLane C.Murrell April 3 1993
very satisfying face climb 4 metres left of *Lichen...*

190 **Scratch** 5.6   `84` N   22m
  FA: K.McLane C.Murrell April 3 1993 [OS]
The crackline just left of *Like it... .*

191 **Lick it in Your Panties** 5.9 *   `84` M   20m
  FA: H.Richardson C.Murrell K.McLane April 3 1993
Start up a short steep crack just right of *Brief Encounter,* pull out to
the right and climb the face above with increasing delight.

192 **Brief Encounter** 5.6   `84` N   22m
  FA: K.McLane April 3 1993 [OS]
Climb the left side of a small pillar and up the crack above.

193 **Tick Crack** 5.7 *   `84` N   22m
  FA: K.McLane April 3 1993 [OS]
The wide layback flake crack 30m left of *Be Happy.* Above the
crack, go left for 3m then straight up.

The Corridor

This is the northern extension of the Fortress East Face where
Shady Valley becomes a narrow canyon. Climbs are described from
the right (north).

❏ **Approach...** See the **Skaha Loop Trail** description.

194 **The Burglar's Dog** 5.10b *   `84` N   15m
  FA: K.McLane R.Barley Sept 27 1992 [OS]
At the very northern end of the Corridor, in the narrowest part of
Shady Valley, is a short tower by the trailside. It sports a good
twisting crack which widens from fingers to fist. Walk off.

195 **The Owl and the Pussycat** 5.10b **   `86` N   35m
  FA: K.McLane R.Barley Sept 27 1992
40m south of *The Burglar's Dog,* up the centre of the wall, is a thin
crackline stepping up through tiny overlaps. Cruxy near the top.
Descend by rappel or walking off to the north.

196 **Sodwrestler** 5.10a *   86 M   2p
FA: R.Barley N.Barley Oct 1992

Start a few metres left of *The Owl and the Pussycat*, at a narrow ramp cutting up to the left. Climb to its top until it is possible to climb the wall above directly, eventually trending right to belay (5.10a). Move up through rounded overlaps, then a step right into a nice crack to finish. (5.9).

197 **Sodwrestler Direct Start** 5.10c *   86 M   10m
FA: R.Barley K.McLane Sept 27 1992

A large fir tree marks the left end of the Corridor. Start just right of the tree and climb a short wall past a FP to join *Sodwrestler*.

The East Face

This is one of the highest and most popular cliffs in the guide, a great sweep of walls and shallow left facing corners. The cliff tapers from 70m at the north end to 12m at the south and is characterised mostly by superb face climbing in the 5.10 - 5.11 grades. Climbs are described from the right (north), the first being beside the big fir tree that marks the demarcation of the East face and the Corridor.

❏ **Approach...** See the **Skaha Loop Trail** description.

198 **Purpendiculous** 5.10c **   86 M   2p
FA: G.Wolkoff S.Chaytor Nov 1989

Behind the big fir tree is a stepped corner about 10m high. Climb it to reach the wall above. Sustained face climbing leads to a belay (5.10b). Continue in a direct line to the top (5.10c).

199 **Primal Dream** 5.10b ***   86 M   2p
FA: G.Wolkoff B.Marchand May 1990

A superb climb. Start 5m left of *Purpendiculous*. Steep face climbing through small overlaps eases after 15m. Turn a roof above on the right, and belay above (5.10b). Exposed face climbing leads to the top (5.10b).

> The wall at the right side of the East Face is undercut by a long 2m overhang. The next 3 climbs all begin here.

200 **By Stealth** 5.11a **   86 M   15m
FA: R.Barley N.Barley Oct 1992

Starts just right of *Fearful in Battle* and joins it after 15m. Rappel.

88

THE FORTRESS EAST FACE

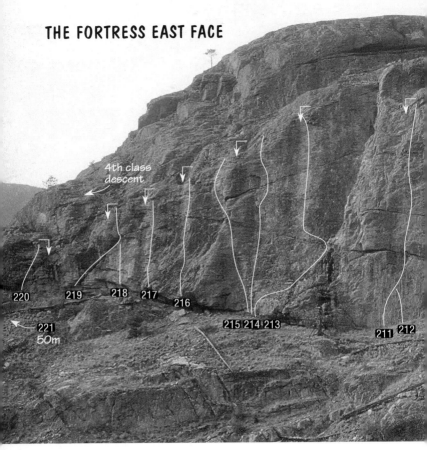

4th class descent

220 221 50m 219 218 217 216 215 214 213 211 212

201 **Fearful in Battle** 5.11b *** **86** M 3p
  FA: (p1) N.Barley R.Barley July 14 1992
  FA: (p2-3) G.Edwards R.Barley (Alts) Sept 24 1992
A splendid climb which weaves its way up the right-hand edge of
the East face. Start at the right side of the overhang and pull over to
gain a thin crack which leads to a small stance below the steep
upper wall (5.11a). Climb the wall above with difficulty, eventually
traversing right to belay (5.11b). Step up left, then climb with less
difficulty to a steep finish (5.10b).

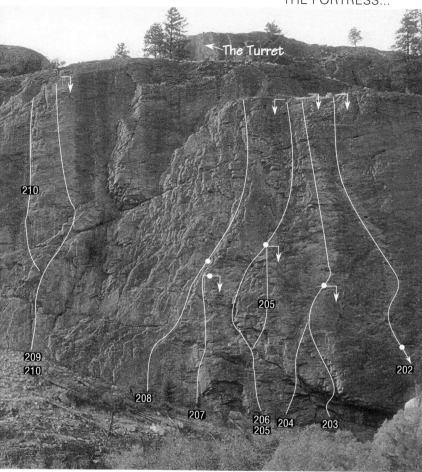

The Turret

210

209
210

208

207

206
205

205

204

203

202

202 **Mortal Combat** 5.11a (3pa) *** 90 86 M 2p
FA: J.Jones R.Barley (Alts) N.Barley (p2 only) Aug 23 1992
A terrific climb. Start just right of the centre of the roof. Strenuous
heaving over the roof leads to a ledge at 15m (5.11a). Climb easily
up leftward then back right with more difficulty to gain a faint
groove and a 3 bolt ladder under the arch above. Weave a delicate
path to the left, then up right, stepping left to finish. A long arduous
pitch, 16qd. (5.11a).

203 **Siege Machine** 5.11b ***   `90` `86`   M   2p
FA: (p1) R.Barley Oct 5 1990
FA: (p2) R.Shackleton P.Shackleton April 1991

A classic, with a magnificent second pitch. Climb through the roof at its left side on good holds to gain a faint, left trending arch. This leads to a crack which is followed with less difficulty to a belay (5.10d). A long pitch of face climbing with occasional rests heads relentlessly for the top (5.11b).

204 **Siege Machine Direct Start** 5.10d *   `90`   M   15m
FA: N.Barley R.Barley Oct 1990
Start 8m to the left and trend up right into the crack.

205 **Special Forces** 5.11a **   `90`   F   30m
FA: R.Barley N.Barley June 14 1992

A direct variation to the first pitch of *For Foot Soldiers*, avoiding the corner. High in the grade.

206 **For Foot Soldiers** 5.10a *   `90`   M   2p
FA: R.Barley N.Barley June 14 1992

Start 8m left of *Seige Machine* and climb up left to gain a prominent left facing corner, undercut at first. The angle eases and the groove leads to a belay (5.10a). Easier climbing to the top (5.9).

207 **Minor Skirmish** 5.10c **   `90`   F   22m
FA: R.Barley R.Shackleton G.Edwards K.McLane March 1991
Good steep climbing. Climb a strenuous open corner to a rest at the top. Long stretches but good rests lead up the wall above.

208 **Et Tu Brutus** 5.9 **   `90`   N   2p
FA: R.Cox S.Cox Sept 3 1989 [OS]

An excellent climb, the easiest route on the East Face taking the right-hand of a series of long grooves curving up to the top of the cliff. Climb the short wall left of *Minor Skirmish* past 3 bolts to the foot of a ramp. Climb this ramp and belay higher (5.9). The corner steepens above, follow it to the top. Exciting and exposed (5.9).

209 **Incomplete Victory** 5.11b **   `90`   M   2p
FA: G.Edwards R.Barley (Alts) March 1991

Climb the initial crack of *Itching to Climb,* then step right at a fork to reach a hidden flake. Belay (5.10b). Hard moves lead up left to a narrow ledge. Sustained climbing leads across orange streaks, then directly up to the top (5.11b).

210 **Itching to Climb** 5.10a * `90` N 45m
FA: R.Cox S.Cox Sept 3 1989 [OS]

A good steep climb up a long, direct corner about 25m left of *Minor Skirmish*. Climb a good, short crack to a horizontal break, then go left easily into the main corner. Scratch your way up the corner, passing an awkward move halfway up.

211 **Storming the Ramparts** 5.10b ** `89` M 40m
FA: N.Barley H.Richardson R.Barley Oct 8 1989

An enjoyable and strenuous climb. Climb a flake crack to a small pedestal, followed by steep laybacking and face climbing to a ledge. Devious final moves lead to a bolt station.

212 **Bend Down and Clip it.** 5.11b * `89` M 8m
FA: D.Hart G.Wong E.Spat 1991

A variation start to *Storming...* up a flake on the right. Easy at first, then a few hard moves gain the pedestal. Easier for tall people.

> The next three climbs all begin at the same place, 10m left of a big broken corner.

213 **The Plum Line** 5.10a *** `89` F 40m
FA: H.Richardson D.van der Torre Sept 29 1989

One of the best climbs at Skaha up a compelling wall capped by a small roof, characterised by good rests, good pro and short cruxes. Climb up to the left end of the ledge below the wall and traverse right to the corner. Move out left onto the wall along a line of good holds, then straight up. A #1-1½ Friend may give moral support halfway up the wall.

214 **Youthful Assault** 5.10b ** `89` M 40m
FA: N.Barley H.Richardson R.Barley Oct 18 1989

Good climbing. Climb easily up the wall into a scoop (3-3½ Friend useful), and move out right below an overlap. Finish up left with delicate moves.

215 **Valiant Veterans** 5.11a ** `89` F 35m
FA: R.Barley R.Collins N.Barley (1pa) July 13 1992
FFA: M.Warwick July 1992

Trend up and left delicately to gain the big wide groove on the left. Turn the overhang above on the left and deal with the final tricky moves up the smooth wall.

216 Typhus 5.10d **   **89** M   30m
FA: R.Barley H.Richardson G.Edwards Sept 23 1992

At the point where the wide groove peters out into the undercut base of the cliff, pull over the lip on good holds, move left and climb directly up the wall. A small Friend may help.

217 The Plague 5.11a **   **89** F   22m
FA: R.Barley A.Barley T.Barley N.Barley April 19 1992

Good technical climbing. Start near a large boulder at the base, pull into a vague groove and climb the wall above.

218 Urushiol 5.11a **   **89** M   18m
FA: R.Barley N.Barley Oct 10 1992

The ochre coloured wall on the left offers hard climbing for 10m past 2 bolts to a move left into the diagonal crack of *Pestilential*.

219 Pestilential 5.10c *   **89** N   25m
FA: R.Barley H.Richardson G.Edwards Sept 23 1992

Jam and clutch up the obvious diagonal crack. To add to the excitement,the real difficulties come near the top.

220 Undermined 5.11a **   **89** M   15m
FA: R.Barley N.Barley April 18 1992

A small but fiercely overhanging bay with a series of excellent holds, some tantalisingly hidden. A #1½ Friend helps at the top.

The South Face

A large slabby face, somewhat disjointed and lacking appeal, except for the lower right side.

❏ **Approach...**   Walk 70m around from the end of the East Face.

221 Yingtong Crack 5.8 *   **89** N   22m
FA: K.McLane R.Barley Sept 27 1992 [OS]

A nice fingery crack rising off the bench.

*Yellowbell
Fritillary*

Kevin McLane on the second ascent of Mrs Palmer (Howie Richardson)

94

Hydro Hill

To the west of the Fortress is a lower, dome shaped hill sporting cliffs on several sides. There are four climbs on the east face.

❏ **Approach...**   Due to adjacent private properties, there is no access to Hydro Hill from the north. **Do NOT approach from this direction.** Approach only from the south end of the Fortress.

❏ From the **Fortress East Face...** Head westward along the wide terrace immediately below the South Face with some occasional scrambling, eventually dropping down into the wide, rocky draw on the west side of the Fortress. Hydro Hill is 100m across the gully, conspicuous by two sets of wooden powerline poles on its top. Walk up the gully 150m to the climbs.

❏ From **Braesyde parking area,** follow the trail until it is possible to walk northward into Hydro Hill gully.

> The first two climbs are the obvious parallel cracks just to the north of the southernmost powerpole.

222 Low Resistance 5.8 **   **96** N   20m
   FA: S.Chaytor G.Wolkoff Aug 27 1989
The left-hand crack.

223 High Voltage 5.10a *   **96** N·   20m
   FA: G.Wolkoff S.Chaytor Aug 27 1989
Deceptively difficult. The right-hand crack.

> The next two climbs are approximately 60-80m further to the north along the wall. They face across to the Fortress.

224 Ohme on the Rock 5.8 *   N   15m
   FA: B.Marchand R.Shaw Aug 27 1989
Thin crack and face climbing protected with small nuts.

225 E-ledge-tricity 5.5   N   15m
   FA: R.Shaw B.Marchand Aug 27 1989
Easy face climbing up small ledges right of *Ohme on the... .*

> Across Hydro Hill Gully, opposite the northern pair of power poles, is an obvious set of left leaning diagonal cracks on the West Face of the Fortress, Start behind a big fir tree.

226 The Leaner 5.11c *   M   30m
  FA: R.Atkinson D.Hart Oct 30 1990
Climb the wall past bolts to the roof, then step down left into the crack. Finger and hand jamming lead to a belay. Take a #2 Friend.

HYDRO HILL

222

223

E-ledge-tricity →
Ohme on the Rock

Braesyde

A futuristic crag with a magnificent aspect overlooking Skaha Lake with the benchlands of the parking area below. There are only two climbs here at present, both of them quite brilliant.

❏ **Approach...**   From the Braesyde parking area, walk up an obvious draw. If approaching from Hydro Hill Gully, contour around on the south side on a high terrace.

Like the parking area below, this crag is on private property and climbing here is by courtesy of the owners. Continued activity is at their discretion, so please act responsibly.

227 Cry Freedom 5.11a ***   **97** M   40m
  FA: R.Atkinson J.Korman R.Barley June 9 1990
The tremendous corner in the middle of the face. Say no more.

228 Sparky Bites 5.12a ***   **97** M   40m
  FA: J.Korman July 1990
The majestic arete left of the corner. Good rests but a difficult crux near the top. Start on the right and follow the arete, teetering on the crest. Occasional hard moves intersperse with rests. All bolts for protection, but a small wire may be useful in the upper part.

BRAESYDE

228 227

Parking

Hydro Hill

Great White Wall

WINDY HILL

Diamond Back

The Wave

Blazing Buttress
Elusive Edge

White Slab

Peach Buttress

Fortress East Face

The Loop Trail

Whitewash Buttress

Shady Valley

Windy Hill

East of the Fortress is a series of open grassy benches rising gently from the south to the north, with many small crags dotting the hillside. A nice place to wander around. The Skaha Loop Trail skirts around Windy Hill on the south and east.

Whitewash Buttress

The most southerly cliff on Windy Hill, sporting some promising walls and one large corner.

❏ **Approach...** See the **Skaha Loop Trail** description.

229 Whitewash 5.11a ** `102` M 30m
   FA: R.Barley N.Barley June 1991

The inviting corner in the middle of the face gives a steep climb. Climb the wall left of the corner, to the crux in the upper dihedral.

White Slab

100m across from the centre of the East Face of the Fortress is a white south facing slab with two vague lines, but lots of holds. The two climbs offer little protection, but belay bolts are on top. The top can be reached by walking up the wide gully on the right.

❏ **Approach...** From Shady Valley hike up a short trail starting from the stand of tall trees south of the East Face of the Fortress.

230 Nice 5.6 * `99` N 20m
   FA: A.Barley solo) April 18 1992 [OS]

The right-hand line. No protection.

231 Easy 5.5 * `99` N 20m
   FA: A.Barley (solo) April 18 1992 [OS]

The left-hand line. No protection

> The next climb is around to the left from White Slab,
> on the wall facing the East Face of the Fortress.

232 Facing the Enemy 5.10c `99` M 3m
   FA: R.Barley N.Barley A.Barley T.Barley April 17 1992

Start at the bottom of the cliff, and climb to the slanting dihedral and follow it until a pull out right is possible. Surmount the bulge and follow the easy wall above.

230
231

View from
Fortress
East Face

Red Tail Wall 100m

Rattlesnake

Peach Buttress

A south facing wall which boasts a striking arete.

❏ **Approach...** On the Loop Trail, 100m East of White Slab.

233 Little Peach 5.7 ***   **99**   N   15m
    FA: A.Barley T.Barley April 19 1992 [OS]

A fine climb up the enticing arete at the right-hand side of the cliff. Easier than it looks, but don't expect much protection.

234 Body Check 5.9 *   **99**   N   18m
    FA: A.Barley T.Barley April 19 1992

A face climb 20m left of *Little Peach*. Not much protection.

> The next climb is well named. Try this... Follow the Skaha Loop Trail north from Peach Buttress to the bottom of the short hill leading up to the south end of Elusive Edge. At this point, walk back south along a lower treed bench for 30m to a noticeable crack on the east facing cliff on the right.

235 Searching for the Holy Flail 5.8   N   15m
    FA: G.Wolkoff R.Cox May 1992 [OS]

A stepped crack up through a bulge to a ledge and an easier finish.

The Wave

Across from Red Tail Wall at the north end of the Fortress is a long, south facing edge with a curious wave-like formation along its top, unclimbed as yet. The climbs are at the extreme left and right ends. This is the biggest crag on Windy Hill.

❏ **Approach...** Can be easily accessed from several directions. From the Skaha Loop Trail at the south end of Elusive Edge, walk along a good trail westward for 100m to the east end of The Wave. From Red Tail Wall, walk down into Shady Valley and up the other side to the west end of the crag.

236 The Dreaded Lurgi 5.11a *   **99**   N   22m
    FA: K.McLane R.Barley Sept 25 1992

At the far west end of the cliff, climb diagonally leftward below an arching roof to an easier crack which leads to the top.

237 Apologies 5.9   **99**   N   15m
    FA: H.Lenney G.Edwards Sept 27 1992

The wide groove right of *The Dreaded...* It eases off higher up.

238 Neddy Seagoon 5.10b *   **99** N   20m
FA: K.McLane G.Edwards Sept 25 1992 [OS]

A steep right facing corner at the east end of the cliff with a small overhang at the top.

Rockpiler

A small, south facing escarpment at the top of Windy Hill which gives an excellent vantage point to survey the area.

❏ **Approach...**   Continue uphill from the east end of The Wave, 40m right of *Neddy Seagoon*, or approach along the benches south and east of East Portal.

239 Little Darling 5.10a **   **102** N   18m
FA: A.Barley (solo) April 18 1992 [OS]

Superb. The obvious arete on the right side. Cruxy at mid-height.

240 Consolation 5.5   **102** N   15m
FA: K.McLane L.McLane Oct 11 1992

A scruffy corner right of the arete.

Elusive Edge

A long east facing cliff in the narrow valley east of Windy Hill. The three climbs are in two locations.

❏ **Approach...**   See the **Skaha Loop Trail** description.

At the south end of Elusive Edge is a small, overhanging wall facing south with a fine jamcrack on its right side. It can be found 50m west of the top of the short hill on the Skaha Loop Trail which leads up to the south end of Elusive Edge. The trail from Red Tail Wall joins the Loop Trail here.

241 Stingo 5.10c **   **102** N   12m
FA: A.Barley T.Barley April 19 1992

The crack on the right side. Beautiful strenuous handjamming.

Walk along the edge for about 150m to an obvious hanging corner rising above the left end of a low roof.

242 The Illusory Megacling 5.10d **   **102** M   22m
FA: R.Barley G.Edwards H.Lenney Sept 28 1992

Climb directly up to the roof and undercling left to gain the corner. Difficult exit moves.

The next climb is on a hidden terrace above *Illusory Mega...*

243 **Elusive Summit** 5.10b * M 20m
FA: *R.Barley N.Barley R.Shackleton Oct 12 1992*

Scramble up an easy ramp that splits the cliff diagonally left of *Illusory Megacling.* Climb the crackline up the centre of the wall.

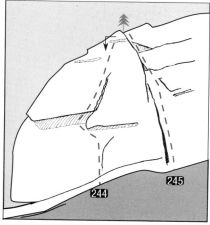

Guy Edwards on the first ascent of A Step Beyond

Blazing Buttress

An impressive south facing wall barely peeping over the trees, with two excellent climbs at opposite ends of the spectrum of difficulty. Check out the west face!

❏ Approach... See the **Skaha Loop Trail** description.

244 A Step Beyond ! 5.11d ***   **102** F   25m
FA: G.Edwards P.Audet (1pa) Sept 1992
FFA: unknown c. April 1993

An impressive line up the centre of the left-hand wall. Pull through a roof to reach an enticing line of sideholds. Cruxy above.

245 Sunspot 5.8 *   **102** N   25m
FA: G.Edwards H.Lenney R.Barley Sept 26 1992 [OS]

The big groove and crack line on the right gives a fine expedition. Keep left to finish.

Diamond Back

East of Windy Hill is the wide, rounded summit of a small dome. On its east side is an impeccable cliff, boasting one of the best climbs at Skaha. Climbs are described from the left (south).

❏ Approach... From **Elusive Edge:** Leave the Skaha Loop Trail at the south end of the cliff, (30m from *Stingo* #241) and follow a trail eastward which leads down into the wide, shallow gully. Continue up the other side, passing a large crag on the left (not a single climb here!) before reaching a crest and dropping down southward through a fine stand of tall ponderosa pine trees. The crag is 200m further on the right, 7 minutes from Elusive Edge.

246 Sidewinder 5.10c **   **105** F   20m
FA: G.Wolkoff R.Cox May 1992

A face climb up to rappel bolts.

247 Easy Prey 5.8 **   **105** N   20m
FA: R.Cox G.Wolkoff May 1992

A small left facing corner which peters out after 15m. Face climbing leads on to a belay above. It is also possible to traverse right lower down and finish up the big corner.

248 Ready to Strike 5.10a ***   **105** M   30m
FA: R.Cox G.Wolkoff May 1992

A magnificent climb up the spectacular corner which cleaves the crag. Just do it!

The next 2 climbs are excellent crack and face routes up the severely undercut wall right of the corner.

249 **Chameleon** 5.10b **   **105**   M   26m
FA: R.Cox G.Wolkoff May 1992

The left-hand crack. Rappel in to a 3 bolt belay to get started. A more direct start has been top-roped.

250 **Viper** 5.10d **   **105**   M   30m
FA: G.Wolkoff R.Cox may 1992

The right-hand crack. Stem up off a so-convenient tree to bypass the undercut, then up right to the crack. Long reaches at the top!

Rappel in   **DIAMOND BACK**

Descent

246

247

248

249

250

Lakeside Cliff

A rambling cliff on Lakeside Road overlooking Skaha Lake. There are only two known routes. This was possibly the first cliff in the Skaha area to see climbing activity.

❏ **Approach...** The cliff is located on Lakeside Road, 9km north of Okanagan Falls, and 5km south of Yorkton Ave in Penticton. Parking is available by the lakeshore.

251 **Bundon's Crack** 5.8   **106** N   2p
FA: unknown (before 1972)

The obvious vegetated crackline up the centre of the cliff. Belay in a sentry box at 35m (5.8). A troublesome exit leads to the top. Belay way back (5.8).

252 **Illegal Alien** 5.9   **106** N   30m
FA: D.Hopkins H.Richardson 1978

18m right of *Bundon's Crack* is a short finger crack midway up the cliff. Reach its base easily from the right. Finish up broken terrain.

LAKESIDE CLIFF

← Penticton

251 252

Lambing Grounds

This is an extensive series of cliffs and gullies rising east of Skaha Lake with its own parking area and approach, 2km south of the Fortress. The land is owned by the Nature Trust of BC and leased to the BC Wildlife Branch of the Ministry of Environment, Lands and Parks for the purpose of ecological protection. The public have access to the lands on foot for quiet enjoyment, but currently there are concerns that an increase in the number of climbers may unduly disturb the wildlife. This is under study. In the meanwhile, the BC Wildlife Branch have requested that climbers observe a voluntary closure from April 1st to June 30th due to the especially high wildlife values in that period. Please observe this closure and any signage posted.

The cliffs listed all lie in a valley running north to south, parallel to Eastside Road. It is the geological extension of Shady Valley.

❏ **Parking...**   Heading south from Penticton on Lakeside Road, Smythe Drive is passed after 3km, then Lakeside Cliff, a further 1.5km. The road then turns to the east into a wide bay at the back of which a gated gravel road cuts back sharply to the north. Park here, 0.9 km south of Lakeside Cliff. If driving north from Okanagan Falls, it is approximately 8km. Do not block access.

❏ **All approaches...**   Walk northward up the gravel road, then steeply up a track to the top of a bench. Trend up right here to rejoin the road. It winds steadily uphill and after 10 minutes levels off and enters a narrow rocky canyon. Talon Wall can be seen ahead on the right, and Echo Wall on the left. For Big Horn Hollow, continue northward for 10 minutes until the road reaches its high point before dropping down over private property into Gillies Creek. Walk a few metres up to the right onto a crest at the edge of a deep, wide gully. From the crest, walk down into Big Horn Hollow traversing north 100m to Haven Crag, facing east. Refuge is another 100m further north up the gully, facing west.

Bunchgrass

Talon Wall

This is a huge rambling cliff 150m high, split by Rattlesnake Ramp, a wide terrace splitting the cliff into upper and lower levels. The cliff generally has a slabby aspect, but also contains considerable amounts of steep rock. Rattlesnake Ramp is a good excursion in its own right, involving minimal scrambling to gain the top of the cliff. All of the climbs listed are below Rattlesnake Ramp on the left-hand wall and are described from the right (south).

❏ **Approach...**   See Lambing Grounds description.

253 Bait 'n Fate 5.10a   **108**   N   10m
  FA: R.Cox G.Wolkoff June 24 1991 [OS]
A short crack hidden behind a tree , 20m right of *STP*.

254 STP 5.10b ***   **108**   M   2p
  FA: R.Cox G.Wolkoff (Alts) May 1992
A terrific climb low in its grade, 30m left of the south end of the lower wall. Climb up 15m of square, stepped overhangs to reach a good crack. Belay near the top of the crack (5.10b). Exposed face climbing leads to Rattlesnake Ramp (5.10b). A large Friend helps.

TALON WALL

257

256

Eagle's Eyrie

Rattlesnake Ramp

258   255

254   253

Parking

108

255 Talon Twister 5.11a **   **108**   M   35m
FA: G.Wolkoff R.Cox July 1991 [OS]

A fine climb which leads up to the ledge of Eagles Eyrie. Start at the very bottom of the huge arch system which borders the crag at its left side. Climb a 5m slab to a crevasse. Pull onto the main wall, bolt protected, to an overlap at 15m. Face climbing and a second overlap lead to Eagles Eyrie.

Starting from the ledge of Eagles Eyrie at the top of *Talon Twister* are 2 climbs which reach up to Rattlesnake Ramp. They are both several grades easier than *Talon Twister* but can be approached by climbing that route or by hiking up Rattlesnake Ramp and rappelling down to Eagles Eyrie.

256 Raptor's Prey 5.9 **   **108**   M   30m
FA: R.Cox G.Wolkoff June 25 1991

From Eagle's Eyrie, climb a short corner above the ledge, trend left above then follow the line of weakness up right to the Ramp.

257 The Griffin 5.10a **   **108**   N   2p
FA: R.Cox G.Wolkoff June 24 1991 [OS]

Good exposed climbing. Head up left from Eagles Eyrie into the prominent corner system. Belay in the corner (5.9). Follow it to the top (5.10a).

258 Thunderbird 5.9 **   **108**   M   3p
FA: R.Cox G.Wolkoff (Alts) May 1991 [OS]

A long adventurous expedition up the huge leaning arch and corner system at the left side of the wall. Start left of the bottom of the corner and face climb past bolts to reach a belay in the corner (5.9). Follow the line! A very long pitch of 50m (5.7) reaches the next belay. The corner above arches out to a blocky finish (5.8).

Echo Wall

This is the attractive 60m cliff which faces east across the valley to the climbs on Talon Wall. It is clearly noted by a grove of tall trees at its base and a line of overhangs up a big slanting fault which marks the right-hand side of the cliff. The grove of trees at the base marks the start of the routes.

❏ **Approach...**   See Lambing Grounds description.

259 Sky Train 5.9 *   M   35m
FA: R.Cox G.Wolkoff Oct 1991 [OS]

Starting at the left side of the grove of trees, climb a chimney then a ramp leading to a ledge. The obvious seam in the face above is marked by a FP. Climb it.

260 Rack and Roll 5.10d *   M   2p
FA: R.Cox G.Wolkoff May 1992 [OS p1]

Near the right side of the grove of trees, climb an obvious right facing, flaring, corner-flake to a belay at its top, a short pitch (5.10a). Continue up and right, some awkward face moves lead past several bolts. Then go up and left over easier ground to join *Sky Train* (5.10d).

Big Horn Hollow

The wide valley leading north from Talon Wall rises gradually to a narrow col before dropping down into Gillies Creek. Cliffs line each side of this col, called Big Horn Hollow. Two cliffs contain routes.

❏ **Approach...**   See Lambing Grounds description.

Haven Crag

An east facing cliff sporting two cracks and a bolted face climb.

261 Having a Bad Hair Day   * 5.9   **111** N   15m
FA: H.Burkhardt S.Chaytor Sept 1990

12m right of the south end of the cliff is a steep, appealing crack with a sentry box at 10m. A hairbrush and mirror may help.

262 Offspring   5.11a   **111** F   25m
FA: G.Wolkoff R.Cox June 1991

A very direct bolted face climb in the centre of the crag.

263 Full Curl   ** 5.10b   **111** N   30m
FA: G.Wolkoff R.Cox Aug1990

The unmistakable left leaning crack in the middle of the cliff.

Refuge

From Haven Crag, descend into the bed of the Big Horn Hollow and traverse northward for 50m to the north end of a steepish cliff and the base of an impressive left facing corner crack.

264 Limited Entry 5.9 **   **111** N   30m
FA: R.Cox G.Wolkoff June 1991 [OS]

The crack passes a bulge at 15m. Easier terrain soon leads up. A
large Camalot was used on the first ascent.

BIG HORN HOLLOW

Talon Wall and Parking

Private Property

Haven

261 262 263

Refuge

264

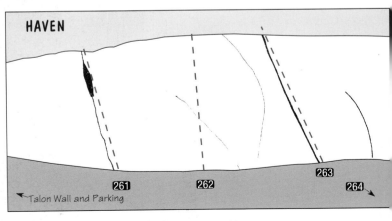

HAVEN

261   262   263   264

Talon Wall and Parking

Alphabetical Index of Climbs and Crags

ALPHABETICAL INDEX

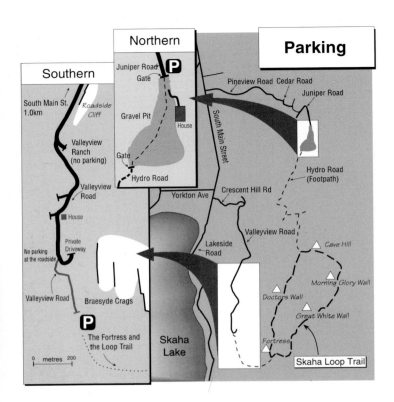

Parking

Northern

Juniper Road
Gate
Gravel Pit
House
Gate
Hydro Road

Pineview Road Cedar Road
Juniper Road
South Main Street
Hydro Road
(Footpath)

Southern

South Main St.
1.0km
Roadside
Cliff

Valleyview
Ranch
(no parking)

Valleyview
Road

House

No parking
at the roadside

Private
Driveway

Valleyview Road

Braesyde Crags

The Fortress and
the Loop Trail

0   metres   200

Yorkton Ave
Crescent Hill Rd

Valleyview Road

Lakeside
Road

Skaha
Lake

Cave Hill

Morning Glory Wall

Doctors Wall

Great White Wall

Fortress

Skaha Loop Trail

117

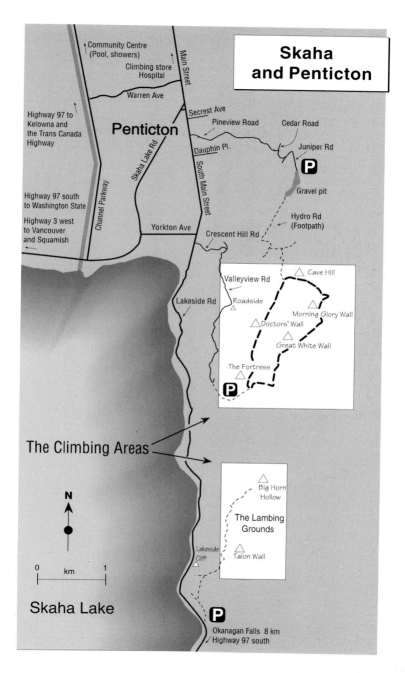

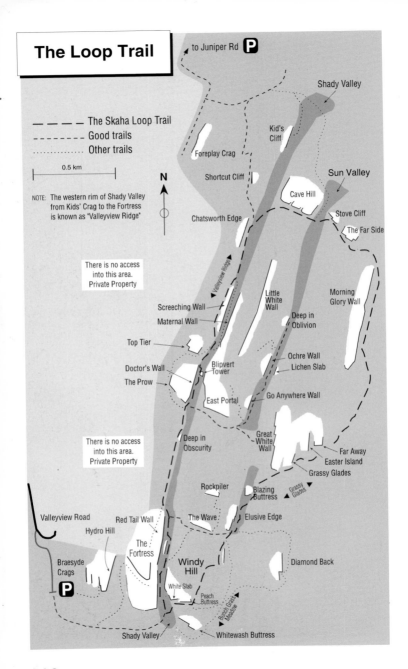

The Loop Trail

to Juniper Rd 🅿

Shady Valley

— — — The Skaha Loop Trail
- - - - Good trails
.... Other trails

|———— 0.5 km ————|

NOTE: The western rim of Shady Valley
from Kids' Crag to the Fortress
is known as "Valleyview Ridge"

Kid's Cliff

Foreplay Crag

Shortcut Cliff

Sun Valley

Cave Hill

Stove Cliff

The Far Side

Chatsworth Edge

Valleyview Ridge

There is no access
into this area.
Private Property

Screeching Wall

Maternal Wall

Little White Wall

Deep in Oblivion

Morning Glory Wall

Top Tier

Doctor's Wall

The Prow

Blipvert Tower

Ochre Wall

Lichen Slab

East Portal

Go Anywhere Wall

There is no access
into this area.
Private Property

Deep in Obscurity

Great White Wall

Far Away

Easter Island

Grassy Glades

Rockpiler

Blazing Buttress

Grassy Glades

Valleyview Road

Red Tail Wall

The Wave

Elusive Edge

Hydro Hill

The Fortress

Windy Hill

Diamond Back

Braesyde Crags

🅿

White Slab

Peach Buttress

Bunch Grass Meadow

Shady Valley

Whitewash Buttress

119

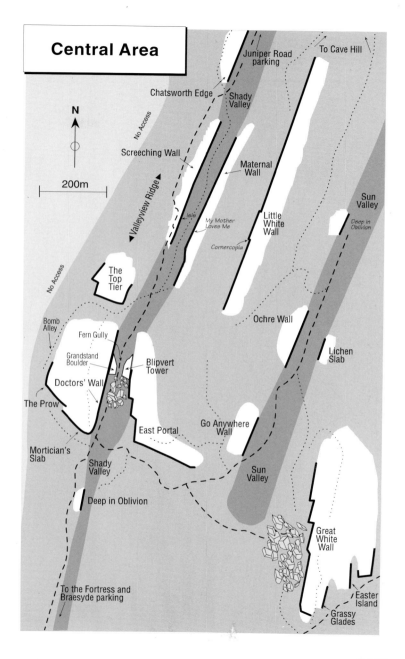

Central Area

N

200m

Juniper Road parking

To Cave Hill

Chatsworth Edge

Shady Valley

Screeching Wall

Maternal Wall

Sun Valley

No Access

Valleyview Ridge

Isis

My Mother Loves Me

Little White Wall

Deep in Oblivion

Cornercopia

The Top Tier

No Access

Bomb Alley

Fern Gully

Grandstand Boulder

Blipvert Tower

Doctors' Wall

Ochre Wall

Lichen Slab

The Prow

Mortician's Slab

East Portal

Go Anywhere Wall

Shady Valley

Sun Valley

Deep in Oblivion

Great White Wall

To the Fortress and Braesyde parking

Easter Island

Grassy Glades

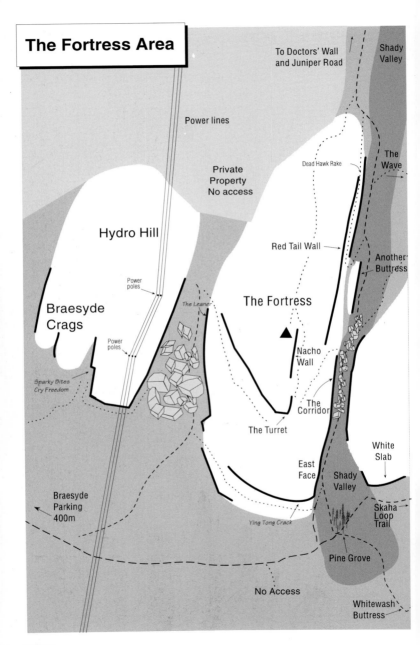

The Fortress Area

To Doctors' Wall and Juniper Road

Shady Valley

Power lines

Private Property No access

Hydro Hill

Dead Hawk Rake

The Wave

Red Tail Wall

Another Buttress

Power poles

The Leaner

Braesyde Crags

The Fortress

Power poles

Nacho Wall

Sparky Bites
Cry Freedom

The Corridor

The Turret

White Slab

East Face

Shady Valley

Braesyde Parking 400m

Skaha Loop Trail

Ying Tong Crack

Pine Grove

No Access

Whitewash Buttress

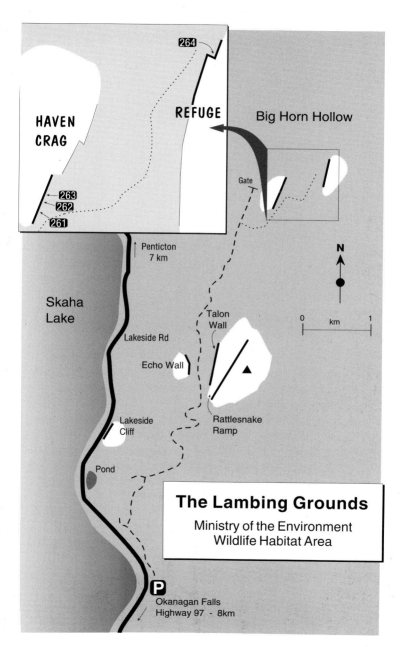

264

HAVEN
CRAG

REFUGE

Big Horn Hollow

Gate

263
262
261

Penticton
7 km

Skaha
Lake

N

0   km   1

Lakeside Rd

Talon
Wall

Echo Wall

Lakeside
Cliff

Rattlesnake
Ramp

Pond

The Lambing Grounds

Ministry of the Environment
Wildlife Habitat Area

P
Okanagan Falls
Highway 97 - 8km

The Tick List

5.5

☐ Big White Dogma		73
☐ E-ledge-tricity		95
☐ Easy	*	98
☐ No Sweat Arete		33
☐ Rat Warren Chimney		36
☐ Sinners in Paradise		72
☑ Steve's		61
☐ The Big Itch		29

5.6

☐ A Day Out with the Boys		33
☑ Be Happy	**	85
☐ Brief Encounter		87
☐ Bull Corner		70
☑ Don't Worry	**	85
☐ Down and Dirty		52
☐ Easy Does It	*	46
☑ Gem Quality	**	37
☐ Hexxus the Horrible		46
☐ Hidden Corner	**	74
☐ Life in the Slow Lane		44
☐ Mellow Yellow		43
☐ Nice	*	98
☐ Scratch		87
☐ Squeezy Stomach	*	74
☐ The Bones	*	79
☐ The Rest is Inconsequ..		64
☐ Tunnel of Love		73

5.7

☐ Bear Shit on a Doorknob		33
☐ Brace Yourself		64
☑ Diamond in the Rough	**	38
☑ Go Here		61
☐ Gollum		85
☐ Little Peach	***	100
☐ Mother's Day		30

☐ Mr. Clean		53
☐ Primus		34
☐ Pure Jam	*	39
☑ Quo Vadis	**	61
☐ Rock up Another One		75
☐ Rose in the Corner		73
☑ Rough Cut	**	40
☐ Snowbirds		44
☐ The Risk is All		84
☐ Tick Crack		87
☐ Uncut	*	40

5.8

☐ 15 Carat	**	40
☐ Bilbo Baggins		85
☐ Bill's Crack	*	35
☐ Bundon's Crack		106
☐ Centre Crack		40
☑ Corporate Bladder	*	61
☐ Deep in Oblivion		63
☐ Dirty with the Money		81
☐ Double Exposure	***	56
☐ Dryathlon		67
☐ Easy Prey	**	104
☐ Ham Shank		43
☑ Lichen in My Panties	**	85
☑ Like it in Her Panties	**	87
☐ Low Resistance	**	95
☐ Ohme on the Rock	*	95
☐ Rat-trap		29
☐ Revolution Tea Party		74
☐ Searching for the Holy...		100
☐ Slacks	**	43
☑ Spring Fingers	**	84
☐ Sunspot	*	104
☐ Tax Burden		33
☐ The Idles of March	**	85
☑ Thinbar	**	84
☑ Tony the Tiger	**	61
☐ Yingtong Crack	*	93

123

5.9

5.10a

5.10b

5.10c

5.10d

5.11a

☐ The Dreaded Lurgi   *   100
☐ Treasure in the Lichen***   80
☐ Unethical   **   47
☐ Urushiol   **   93
☐ Valiant Veterans   *   92
☐ Whine and Dyno   *   30
☐ Whitewash   **   98

5.11b

☐ Ardent   *   29
☐ Bend Down and Clip it*   92
☐ Fearful in Battle   ***   89
☐ Fledgeling   *   59
☐ Grin and Bear It   **   51
☐ Incomplete Victory   **   91
☐ Lion's Lair   *   42
☐ Mortal Combat   ***   89
☐ My Mother Loves Me**   42
☐ Naturopath   **   51
☐ Siege Machine   ***   91
☐ Swami'sPair-a-dice   28
☐ Wings of Desire   ***   65

5.11c

☐ Ankleduster   **   65
☐ Early Bird   *   60
☐ H   ***   80
☐ Hunting Humans   **   42
☐ Iga Uga Chaga Dub   *   29
☐ Isis in Chains   ***   40
☐ Misdiagnosed   **   47
☐ Test of the Ironman   ***   67
☐ The Leaner   *   96

5.11d

☐ A Step Beyond!   **   104
☐ Diamond on the Roof*   80
☐ Disparu   ***   55
☐ Doctor Megatrip   ***   48

☐ Isis   ***   40
☐ Peaches   **   43
☐ The Future is Now   ***   51
☐ The Painted Bird   *   68
☐ Tierdrops   ***   80

5.12a

☐ Acid Test   ***   67
☐ Sparky Bites   ***   96

5.12c

☐ Snakeskin Tracksuit *   62

Stop Press

A number of first ascents have been made recently which were not possible to include in the main body of route descriptions. A brief description is given here. None of the climbs have been checked, so you take your chances with grades and locations.

Rap it Down, Chop it up 5.12b   F
FA: G.Foweraker L.Eltis April 24 1993
This climb is an arete on the west face of the Top Tier. Approach from the South Face, along a vague trail about 40m out from the cliff face. The climb is about 100m north of *Slacks,* and reportedly good. 4qd. Difficulty is up to 5.11b with a hard crux.

Subterranean Homesick Blues 5.11c   N
FA: S.Jeffrey April 18 1993
The thin overhanging crack right of *Basement Abortion* on the north side of Grandstand Boulder.

Rattle and Hum 5.9   N
FA: G.Wolkoff B.Marchand R.Shaw April 1993
A thin crackline squeezed between *Ready to Strike* and *Easy Prey* at Diamond Back. Continue to the rappel station on *Easy Prey.*

No Name 5.11a   M
FA: G.Wolkoff R.Cox May 12 1993
On Echo Wall in the Lambing Grounds. This is a thin slanting crack 10m right of *Rack and Roll* which diagonals up to the right. Gear to 2", TCU's and wires. 2 bolts, 2 cruxes. Rappel down. A single 50m rope may just make it.

❑   The following five climbs are all in the Easter Island area.

Kohmeini Bacon 5.7   N
FA: D.Jones K.McLane May 9 1993
Easter Island. 10m left of the log butting into the centre of the cliff is an obvious left facing flaky corner. Climb it, moving right to finish.

Lesbian Pope 5.9   N
FA: D.Jones K.McLane May 9 1993
Easter Island. The left trending crack right of the corners and the first climb left of Blood on the Tracks. Face climb to finish.

Black Hand of God 5.10c   N
FA: D.Jones D.Serl P.Oxtoby J.Schuppli may 15 1993
Easter Island. Climb the left trending shallow crack which starts about 2m right of Black Mass. Small RPs and TCUs. 25m. Good.

Koresh Barbecue 5.10a   N
FA: D.Jones P.Oxtoby May 23 1993

Easter Island. Follow the line of weakness and cracks on the right-hand edge of *Kohmeini Bacon*, 3m left of *Jumpin' for Jesus*.

Reprobate 5.10b   M
FA: D.Jones P.Oxtoby May 23 1993

Far Away. 25m uphill (north) of *Question Authority*. Climb thin edges to a small alcove, then follow a thin crack up the gently overhanging wall to a second, smaller alcove below the top. 3 bolts.

❏ The next three climbs are on Overly Hanging Out, a small, predominately overhanging crag about 100m northeast of Question Authority on Far Away. The cliff is noted by three large pine trees on a ledge at the base.

Hot Tin Roof 5.6   M
FA: D.Jones P.Oxtoby May 23 1993

Follow the obvious corner at the base of the arete until able to climb more directly on the upper south edge of the overhanging wall. Much easier than it looks. 2 bolts.

Bone Machine 5.10c   M
FA: P.Oxtoby D.Jones May 23 1993

Begin at a crack formed by a semi-detached block. Stretch for the holds above the first bolt and then launch out on good holds over the overhang until able to gain the upper slab which is climbed to a bolt belay. Excellent climbing.

Consenting Adults 5.10c   M
FA: D.Jones P.Oxtoby May 23 1993

Start 3m left of *Bone Machine*. Climb gracefully on jugs and small holds past 2 bolts to a good ledge, then on large jugs over the overhang to the upper slab and a common finish with *Bone Machine*.

❏ The next climb is on the lower tier of Red Tail Wall.

Wildlife Crossing 5.10b   F
FA: D.Jones P.Oxtoby May 24 1993

10m left of *The Risk is All*. Climb the steep slab trending left over a slight bulge split by an incipient crack to reach Dead Hawk Rake. 5 bolts.

❏ The following climb is on China Wall, which is actually the west face of Easter Island. Access is gained by walking up the gully between Grassy Glades and Easter Island.

Tso Ba 5.10a/b   M
FA: P.Oxtoby D.Jones May 24 1993

Climb twin cracks until able to undercling the obvious right trending roof. Exit on good holds at the right-hand end of the roof. 2 bolts.

❏ The next two short climbs are gained by walking up the gully north of Grassy Glades (left of *Sinners in Paradise*) to an obvious flake.

Acadian Flake 5.7   N
FA: C.Comeau J.Schuppli P.Oxtoby May 15 1993   This route was possibly climbed by H.Richardson and D.Hetherington in 1988

The flake. Tree belay, rappel off. Worth a look.

How Could You? 5.6   N
FA: J.Schuppli P.Oxtoby May 15 1993   This route was possibly climbed by H.Richardson and D.Hetherington in 1988

3m left of *Acadian Flake*. The blocky crack topped by a cruxy chimney.

❏ The next 2 climbs are reached by walking up the gully past Easter Island to the south end of a high massif.

Boulder then Barbie 5.6   N
FA: P.Oxtoby solo. May 16 1993

An offwidth crack in a huge south facing corner.

Reaching Juanita 5.9   F
FA: P.Oxtoby D.Jones May 24 1993

Up a flake line one metre left of *Boulder then Barbie*. Good.

Lichen in My Bellybutton 5.7   F
FA: G.Hill H.Lenney May 16 1993

Start in Fern Gully beside Grandstand Boulder and climb a steep arete up to the base of *Granola Bar*.

Short and Kurly 5.12a   F
FA: D.Hart R.Atkinson May 15 1993

In the gully between Hydro Hill and the Fortress are several large square blocks. This climb is up the southeast arete of the largest block.